As a single parent, you need direction and encouragement to help you through the difficulties you face each day. Here you'll receive the comforting advice you need, written by someone who's been there. Virginia Watts Smith shares the struggles...joys...pain... and happy moments she's experienced while raising four children alone. And she also gives you practical help, insights, and enlightening Bible verses that will meet your needs today. You'll find:

- *A list of nationwide singles' fellowship groups and ministries*
- *Educational, financial, and vocational resources available to you*
- *A Single Parent's Inventory that allows you to measure your personal growth*
- *Creative outlets for your family*

and much, much more

Most importantly, Virginia Watts Smith shows you that you're not alone — God's loving presence is *always* with you!

The Single Parent

Virginia Watts Smith

Fleming H. Revell Company
Old Tappan, New Jersey

"Forgive Us," by Pollyanna Sedziol reprinted by permission of ETER-NITY Magazine, Copyright 1975, The Evangelical Foundation, 1716 Spruce St., Philadelphia, Pa. 19103.

Quotations from *Whatever Became of Sin?* by Karl Menninger used by permission of Hawthorn Books, Inc. from WHATEVER BECAME OF SIN? Copyright © 1973 by Karl Menninger, M. D. All rights reserved.

Unless otherwise identified, Scripture quotations are from the King James Version of the Bible.

Scripture quotations identified TLB are from The Living Bible, Copyright © 1971 by Tyndale House Publishers, Wheaton, Illinois 60187. All rights reserved.

Library of Congress Cataloging in Publication Data

Smith, Virginia Watts.
    The single parent.

    "Power book."
    Includes bibliographies.
    1. Single parents—United States. 2. Parenting—United States—Religious aspects—Christianity. I. Title.
HQ755.8.S64 1983   306.8′56   82–16538
ISBN 0–8007–5105–1

Contents

Preface

The traditional household is vanishing—rapidly vanishing! These words scream out at us everywhere we turn.

"Our most cherished institution, the American family, is changing so rapidly that some families have become barely recognizable," says Diane Weathers in her article, "The New American Families" (*Family Circle,* October 7, 1980). "At one time," she continues, "the typical American family was considered to be a husband in the labor force, a wife at home and their children."

In their book, *The Nation's Families: 1960-1990,* George Masnick and Mary Jo Bane present more evidence of the vanishing traditional family, predicting that the so-called family of father, mother, and young children will constitute just over one-fourth of all households by 1990.

One of the most convincing illustrations regarding this drastic change in family structure was noted as delegates to the first of three White House Conferences on Families attempted to define "a family." A subgroup debated the issue, with conservatives defining a *family* as "a group related by marriage, blood or legal custody." Others, including a gay-rights spokesman, called for defining a *family* as "any group that shares common values and a commitment to the future." Delegates left that conference without a definition of a *family,* simply because no agreement could be reached.

University of Chicago professor Philip Hauser noted in a

1977 *Chicago Tribune* article, "The traditional family unit appears to have made way for an increasing number of permutations."

Whether we agree or disagree with these and other evaluations, the alternative family is probably here to stay. With that in mind, let's consider various "family" arrangements as they exist today:

I Living-Together Arrangement

While living together often culminates in marriage, it is also a permanent life-style for some. The number of unmarried couples tripled in ten years, bounding from 523,000 in 1970 to 1,560,000 in 1980. Some 424,000 children under fifteen years of age lived in these households of unmarried couples.

II One-Person Households

Daniel Yankelovich, in his book *New Rules: Searching for Self-Fulfillment in a World Turned Upside Down,* said, "There are fewer typical families than there are households consisting of a single person—the fastest growing category of households reported by the United States Census."

The number of persons living alone grew from 10.9 million in 1970 to 17.8 million in 1980—almost 6.8 million men and over 11 million women.

III The Single Parent

The number of children living with single parents grew from 8.199 million in 1970 to 12.162 million in 1980—an increase of almost 4 million children. Research indicates that nearly one-half of children attending school in the next decade will come from one-parent homes, and half of all today's babies will live in a female-headed household at some time before they reach eighteen.

Heads of single-parent families have been in the past primarily widowed, divorced, or separated. With the sexual revolution came increasing numbers of teenage pregnancies, resulting in over a million children now being raised by teenage unmarried mothers. An additional 1.6 million children currently live with mothers who were teens when they delivered. In the state of Illinois alone there were around 50,000 teenage pregnancies in 1981, and the city of Chicago reported some 13,000. Nationally, 94 to 96 percent of all teenage unwed mothers keep their babies.

But an entirely new group of people has emerged: Those who want to single parent, by choice, not circumstances, and we find growing numbers of single men and women adopting children.

Finally, single parenting has become a (very controversial) possibility through new medical and scientific techniques.

These varied groups of single parents are statistically defined in charts A and B below:

Chart A

Children under 18 living with mothers only as of March, 1980.

Single (never married)	1,721,000
Husband absent (separated)	3,519,000
Widowed	1,260,000
Divorced	4,630,000
	11,130,000

Chart B

Children under 18 living with fathers only as of
March, 1980.

Single (never married)	75,000
Wife absent (separated)	281,000
Widowed	172,000
Divorced	503,000
	1,031,000

IV Transitional Families

According to the *Chicago Tribune,* April 6, 1980, more
than 26 million adults were stepparents, and 18 million children under age eighteen were stepchildren. Naturally, these
transitional (or reconstructed) families may overlap with
family arrangements already noted. The drastic increase in
divorce and remarriage is largely responsible for these complicated living arrangements. But transitional families do
not necessarily improve or stabilize the situation, because 40
percent of second marriages end in divorce (and many of
these partners may marry a third time) as compared to 33
percent dissolution of first marriages. It's striking that five
out of six men (87 percent) and three out of four women (75
percent) remarry within three years.

As a result, growing numbers of children are involved,
interacting with two biological parents and one or more
stepparents, so that children are increasingly becoming
members of more than one household.

Whatever our feelings are concerning these family groups
sprouting up side by side with more traditional families, we
must accept their existence as a fact of life. Not only must

we acknowledge their existence, but their potential must be built upon. For the Christian church, this is a challenging new frontier. The diversity of life-course variables among human beings created by God demands an intensive and critical reexamination of God's message of love, forgiveness, and hope to this world.

While I could suggest reasons for the changes taking place in the families of our country—such as the new morality and loss of faith in the American dream—and I could speculate as to what family life will be in fifty years, the purpose of this book is to try to find the best in, and make the best of, family arrangements we have today, especially single-parent families. It is my hope that not only single-parents and their children, but also ministers, counselors, teachers, family and friends will discover understanding, help, and *hope* through the pages of *The Single Parent.*

I can write of hope because I have a God of hope. In a world where gloom is perpetuated, we must constantly review history, recognizing and acknowledging God, who created the universe. "He . . . hangeth the earth upon nothing," we read in Job 26:7. The world we live in has been whirling around in space with the same orderliness and precision with which God originally set it in motion.

I must reason logically, then, that if the world revolves without effort, cannot I, as God's special creation, trust my Creator? To God my life is a finished book. ". . . We spend our years as a tale that is told," according to Psalms 90:9. It is opened to today's page of my life—spread out before God, my Heavenly Father. But He knows what is written on each page for the rest of my life.

Life is not a game of chance, played in a huge world casino where we are whirled about, stopping and starting without purpose. It should be, rather, a life of God-ordered purposefulness.

The story of Esther in the Bible is exciting. Esther was an orphan being raised by her cousin Mordecai. He posed a haunting question to Esther, during a time of personal crisis: "Who knows but you were born for just such a time as this?" Esther responded with those spine-tingling words, "If I perish, I perish!" (*See* Esther 4:14, 16.) The threatening circumstances surrounding her did not deter her. She was confident and positive, knowing she could trust God, her Creator.

Just so, we also stand before God as individuals. He does not look upon us as wives, husbands, mothers, fathers, sons, daughters—or single parents. No, He sees us as individuals—persons—created to be uniquely ourselves.

God delights in taking impossible situations and turning them into positive experiences.

Of Abraham it was said: "Who against hope believed in hope. . . . He staggered not at the promise of God through unbelief; but was strong in faith, giving glory to God; And being fully persuaded that, what he had promised, he was able also to perform" (Romans 4:18, 20, 21).

Maybe God is just waiting for you, as a single parent, to step out into a life of faith—to "hope when there seems to be no hope."

You can trust God!

The Single Parent

Virginia Watts Smith

And Jesus called a little child unto Him, and set him in the midst of them, And said.... whoso shall receive one such little child in my name receiveth me.

Matthew 18:2, 3, 5

1
Today's Single Parent

Major changes in the family have spawned what might be considered a revolution in child rearing. As we've already discovered, millions of children are being raised in single-parent families, living-together arrangements, and transitional families.

Old Testament references (Exodus 22:22, Deuteronomy 10:18) indicate that widows and orphans were present even early in human history. Widows are probably the first known "single parents" and have remained the number-one contributors to single parenting until very recent years.

More recently, however, due to spiraling divorce rates, the divorced single parent has come to the forefront. In 1980, for example, 4,630,000 children were being raised by divorced women. Suddenly, divorced fathers are flexing their legal muscles and are demanding equal rights for divorced dads. As a result, in 1980, 503,000 children under eighteen were living with their fathers, and organizations such as Fathers United for Equal Rights were surfacing. Yet while times are changing, the *Chicago Tribune* reported in 1982 that, "paternal custody is still seen as an aberration rather than an alternative."

On the other hand, some mothers are simply giving up custody of their children, for a myriad of reasons, adding numbers to the ranks of children already living with their fathers. In 1981 an organization known as Mothers Without Custody was founded in Boston, Massachusetts. The group has 135 chapters and approximately 700 members. Of the organization's members, 85 percent have voluntarily given up custody, 8 percent have lost their children in litigation, 5 percent have been stolen, and state agencies have taken the remaining 2 percent.

But the most recent phenomenon in single parenting may be seen in the increasing numbers of never-married singles, both male and female, who are already single parents or are in the process of becoming one through adoption. There is a definite trend toward single parenthood by choice, not circumstances. For these, becoming a single parent is not like giving birth to a barbed wire fence, but rather a joyful experience.

In the past adoption by singles would have been considered unthinkable by most agencies. As single parenting has become relatively commonplace and since large numbers of children are permanently separated from their families, being shifted from foster homes and institutions, adoption agencies are more willing to allow singles to adopt, hoping to give some permanency to these needy children. Though it takes time and determination, single-parent adoption can be accomplished, and according to the Committee for Single Adoptive Parents, "Many hundreds of single men and women across the United States have adopted children in the last several years."

No state legally forbids adoption by single persons. Some states, however, limit adoption because of the age of the prospective parent, difference in age between parent and child, and duration of residence. The majority of single adoptive parents are women, but adoption by single males is climbing at a slow but steady pace.

In the United States the number of adoptive parents far outweighs the number of children available. For this reason, adoption agencies consider married couples first and only seek a single adoptive parent should a suitable couple not be found. Usually singles are assigned older, minority, physically or emotionally handicapped children, or siblings the agency does not want to separate.

One of the most important criteria for placing children in singles' homes is their relationship with their extended families. Positive extended family support helps both parent and child in the adoptive adjustment. Generally, single adoptive parents have had positive response from parents, other relatives, and neighbors. Interestingly, friends have been less likely to respond positively, especially friends of single male parents.

Agencies tend to select older singles (thirty to forty) mainly because they have acquired sufficient resources and reached a greater level of maturity. Many single adoptive parents live in cities, have higher levels of education, and may be in occupations such as education and social work, which make them more knowledgeable about adoptive children both before and after the adoption.

Though single-parent adoption is still in the research stage, it appears that singles who are interested in and pursue adoption possess "high commitments to parenting." Phyllis Edderly is one of these single adoptive parents who believes that a dedicated, selfless commitment to parenting is absolutely essential. Phyllis owns her own successful company in a large city and lives in a suburb. In 1975 she adopted two girls, one five years old, the other thirteen months. I recently contacted Phyllis again and confirmed her continuing joy and satisfaction as a single parent and her children's successful growth and development.

Phyllis would not encourage other singles to adopt. "It is just too difficult," she says. "Most singles have no idea how difficult parenting is, and to begin with, at least, for many the motive to adopt is a selfish one." When she began the process for adoption, she shared with the agency that she personally had a great desire to parent. She soon discovered that the agency was much more concerned about the adoptive child's welfare and needs than they were for her "great desire to parent." In all honesty, she had to rethink her motive for wanting to adopt. "One can no longer indulge oneself in 'singleness,'" she concludes.

Though Phyllis would not encourage other singles to adopt, she would not change her situation in any way: "It's been worth all the difficulties I've had to have my two beautiful girls."

One of the major problems single adoptive parents face, according to Phyllis, is that there is no allowance to recycle into the mainstream of social life, and that if she were not so busy and satisfied with both her children and business, she would be a very lonely person. Society has generally accepted her black children. Her local Christian community, unfortunately, has been somewhat less than accepting.

In talking with a social worker in Denver, Colorado, I learned that about 5 percent of her agency's yearly total adoptions are given to singles. For example, in 1981, the agency placed ten children with singles—eight with single women, two with single men. These ten single adoptive parents meet together once a week as a support group. Their major problems seem to be in the area of time management and lack of privacy. Time management is a problem we all face—single or married—and requires personal evaluation and discipline. (For helpful resource material on time management, consult chapter twelve.) Newly adopted children tend to cling and invade space the single enjoyed prior to the adoption. As the child becomes less clinging and demanding, the single parent learns to adjust and accept privacy time allotted him.

The most important factor in single adoption (or any adoption) is finding stability for adoptive children who have known little or no stability in their lifetimes. Researchers have found that children in single adoptive homes often have problems when first placed, and adjustment usually takes longer than in married couples' homes. The reason for this difference in adjustment time appears to be largely due to the fact that children placed in single adoptive homes are usually older and come with handicaps. Both children and parents already have much to overcome as they begin the relationship. As time passes, however, and as loving guidance is given, these differences in adjustment seem to fade.

Though the adoption picture has greatly changed over the years, research always requires time. Additional studies on the subject of single-person adoption will continue to examine objective indicators of adjustments such as school records and psychological test scores of children in both single-parent and two-parent homes.

After one study, a report was published stating: "In the thirty-six cases studied we strongly believe that the children involved have found true 'familiness.' " Integrating a lonely child into "familiness" is indeed a worthy goal.

In this less-than-ideal world, our desire must always be to care for needy, waiting children in the best possible way.

Jesus confronted His disciples on one occasion when they wanted to send the children away by saying, "Suffer [let] the little children to come unto me, and forbid them not; for of such is the kingdom of God" (Mark 10:14).

While adoption by a single person may be difficult, and though some may not be in agreement with single-person adoption, for the mature Christian single, adoption can be a potentially rewarding ministry.

Suggested Reading

Berman, Claire. *We Take This Child.* New York: Doubleday, 1974.

Carson, Ruth. *So You Want to Adopt a Child.* New York: Public Affairs Pamphlet.

Jewett, Claudia. *Adopting the Older Child.* Harvard, Mass.: Harvard Common Press, 1979.

Kravik, Patricia. *Adopting Children with Special Needs.* Riverside, Calif.: North American Council on Adoptable Children, 1976.

Livingston, Carole. *Why Was I Adopted?* Secaucus, N.J.: Lyle Stuart, 1978.

Raymond, Louise. *Adoption and After.* Rev. ed. Colette Taube. Dywasuk. New York: Harper & Row, 1974.

U.S. Department of Health and Human Services, *Single Parent Adoption,* #OHDS, 81-30306. Free copy sent on request.

North American Council on Adoptable Children. *Who Has the Right to Know?* Riverside, Calif.: NACAC, 1979. Symposium of articles dealing with the sealed-records question. Write: NACAC, 3900 Market Street, Suite 247, Riverside, California 92501.

So a setback, a serious check, the crumbling of a whole majestic world, may be the necessary road to a renaissance. For each of us, a setback can become the opportunity of a return to oneself and a personal meeting with God.

PAUL TOURNIER
Guilt and Grace

2
The Unmarried Parent

For many women, hearing the doctor say "You're pregnant" can be one of life's most exciting moments. For others, like Linda, an unmarried seventeen-year-old, those words brought bewilderment, heartache, despair, and then a painful decision. The day after Linda delivered her baby girl, she wrote the following letter:

My dear, precious baby daughter,

I wanted to write this letter to you in hope that someday when you are old enough to understand, you might read this letter and know how much I love you.

Yesterday, January 28, 1981, at 7:17 A.M., I gave birth to a beautiful baby girl. You were so soft and cuddly. I wished that things had been different, but I couldn't change that. It was because I loved you so much I came to the decision to give you up to a mommy and daddy who would be able to love you and give you a complete home. This is something I could not provide, being a single parent. You deserve the very best. I know that God will give you a mommy and a daddy who will love Jesus and tell you of His great love for you. Precious daughter, as I look to the years ahead, it is my prayer that you will ask Jesus into your heart at an early age and then live for Him forever. If we never meet

down here on earth, it is my prayer we will meet in Heaven.
I want you to know, also, that I asked Jesus in my heart October 15, 1980.

In closing, this is my prayer:

> I said a prayer today for you
> And asked the Lord above
> To keep you safely in His love.
> I didn't ask for fortune,
> For riches or for fame
> I only asked for blessings
> In the Savior's Holy name.
> Blessings to surround you
> In times of trials and stress
> And inner joy to fill your heart
> With peace and happiness.

> Lovingly,
> YOUR MOTHER

Linda is just one of over a million teenage girls who become pregnant each year. Nationally, 94 to 96 percent of these teenage mothers keep their babies—often children raising children.

Teenage pregnancy has become a devastating problem in our nation and knows no racial or socioeconomic barriers. In fact, the United States has one of the highest teenage birth rates in the industrialized world.

Dr. Donald Dye, director of maternal and child health programs for the Chicago Department of Health describes the situation as "an awful social problem. It's the beginning of the poverty cycle. There's a high incidence of child abuse and it's a major contributor to high infant mortality rates, especially those babies who die after hospital discharge." When I talked with Dr. Dye on the telephone, he stated, "I unequivocally stand by the statement I made for the *Chicago Tribune* article in May, nineteen eighty-one, and unfortunately, the situation is no better in nineteen eighty-two."

Suzanne Hinds, former chairperson of the Illinois Caucus on Teenage Pregnancy adds emphasis to Dr. Dye's statement, saying, "I don't think we've come anywhere close to solving the problem. Nobody knows what to do."

Men and women of all ages are daily confronted with questions and decisions regarding sexual morality. Teenagers, however, seem especially vulnerable to pressures from society, whether those pressures come from media, peers, or other sources. Music for teenagers is often explicitly worded, for example, "Take Your Time (Do It Right)" or "Do That to Me One More Time." Clothing manufacturers encourage sex by showing advertisements with teenagers, in jeans, astride each other. Movies and television exploit teenage sex, making it appear glamorous, necessary, and even right.

One sixteen-year-old from Palo Alto, California, reflected, "It must have been a lot easier when society set the standards for you. It can get awfully complicated. I guess that's the price we have to pay for freedom" (*Newsweek,* September 1, 1980). Underneath the veneer and sophistication of many adolescents, there is indeed doubt, conflict, and confusion. Sex education has proven to be of negligible value, and despite instruction in birth control and use of contraceptives, much ignorance remains on the subject of sex.

Peer pressure is probably at the top of the list of causes for the dramatic rise in teenage pregnancy. In some neighborhoods, pregnancy has almost become a status symbol. Teenagers, on the one hand, are noted for their rebellion; and on the other hand, they fiercely conform with their peers. Immediate self-gratification and lack of responsibility also appear to be major factors in teenage sex.

Sometimes teenagers even believe pregnancy will:

1. *Solve problems at home.* "I fought with my parents and thought if I had a baby things would change."
2. *Provide love.* "A baby would need and love me. It would be mine."
3. *Get me away from school.* "I hated school."
4. *Make me an adult and provide freedom.* "I can do what I want to do, when I want to, and how I want to."
5. *Encourage self-esteem.* "I am my own person."

In spite of these lofty expectations, seldom do positive changes take place. Rather, life usually becomes more complicated and depressing.

Many people other than the unmarried mother are also adversely affected (including the biological father, grandparents, other relatives, friends, schools, churches, and ultimately cities, states, and our nation). But the persons most adversely affected are the unmarried mother and her child. Some of the special problems the mother (and sometimes the father) may face are:

1. *Maternal death risk.* Death risk is 60 percent higher for younger teenagers than for women in their twenties.

2. *Suicide.* Suicide rate for teenage mothers is seven times higher than the rate for teenagers without children.
3. *School dropout.* Pregnancy is the most common cause of school dropout among young women.
4. *Abortion.* There were 2.2 million abortions in the United States between 1972–1978. Teenagers account for more than 30 percent of all abortions performed during that period of time.
5. *Divorce/separation.* Sixty percent of pregnant teenage brides are divorced or separated within six years of marriage.
6. *Poverty.* Families with young children headed by mothers aged 14–25 are seven times as likely to live below the poverty level.
7. *Decision to keep or relinquish child.* The decision to keep or relinquish the baby must be made as objectively as possible, with the child, the mother, and sometimes the father in mind.

Some special problems the babies of unmarried teenage parents face are:

1. *Infant mortality.* Such children are two to three times more likely to die within their first year.
2. *Health problems.* These children are twice as likely to be premature, suffer from birth injury, childhood illnesses, retardation, and other neurological defects.
3. *Child abuse.* A higher incidence of child abuse exists among teenage parents.

If you are young, unmarried, and pregnant (or already mothering a baby), you undoubtedly relate to what has been said. It's very easy for others who are not in your situation to offer advice, consolation, and perhaps support—well-intentioned to be sure. Sadly, verbal comments are seldom helpful, especially now. Your mind is probably spinning with doubts and questions—important and valid questions that require answers:

> How can I care for a baby financially, emotionally, and physically?
>
> Where will I live before the baby is born? after the baby is born?
>
> Should I, or could I, live at home?
>
> Will my family and friends reject me?
>
> Will I ever date again, and if I do, what will the fellow think of my having a baby?
>
> Do I really want to be "tied down" to a baby and all the responsibilities having a child brings?
>
> Should I return to school?
>
> Can I get a job that will pay enough to make it worthwhile to work?
>
> Who can I talk to who will be understanding and kind, yet objective, and help me get started on a new life?
>
> Should I give my baby up for adoption?
>
> What is best for me and my baby?
>
> What responsibility does the biological father have? Should I marry him?

These are heavy questions and burdens for a young person to bear. Somewhere along the way the glamour of sex seems to have faded into a nightmare. It no longer is, "Oh, everybody's doing it!" It now becomes very personal! *You* are the one who is experiencing guilt, isolation, anxiety, and frustration.

One of the most crucial decisions you must make is in relation to the future of your child. All alternatives must be considered in order to make the best possible decision.

Linda, a more mature unmarried mother, decided in favor of adoption, but not without struggle. She confided, "I had such guilt. I went through hell. Then I began to experience forgiveness such as I had never known. I knew God had forgiven me." She then faced another crisis: "What will I do with the baby? It was the most difficult decision I ever made," she said. "I was very alone and experienced awful feelings. Then I began to realize that this baby was God's child, not mine. The world glibly speaks of love—love to give in order to get. Now I know just a little bit about God's sacrificial love. I was adopted into God's family, and now I'm adopting my child into a Christian home. It still hurts, but I know it is best for me and my child."

Sara and Jean, on the other hand, decided to keep their babies. Sara had the help of her sister and brother-in-law throughout the pregnancy and after the baby was born. She continues to live with her sister and family in a large old house adapted to the special needs of two families under the same roof. Both Sara and her child benefit from the strength of the larger unit. There are child-care trade-offs, shared household chores, and companionship for the adults and the two children involved.

Jean married Jim, the father of her child. Both had been good students and were very talented. After Jean became pregnant and had her child, both Jean and Jim dropped out of school: Jean, because of many responsibilities at home and with the baby; and Jim because he had to work two jobs. Despite their valiant efforts, they simply could not make it financially. A couple of weeks before their baby was two years old, they separated, went back to their own homes, and returned to school. Jim later said, "I love my wife and baby. I wish we had waited. I'm sure we could have made it."

It's good to know that when questions arise and decisions must be made there are organizations who really do care and can help find answers to difficult problems. These organizations provide professional and spiritual counseling, help with living arrangements, prenatal and hospital care, education and job opportunities, budget planning, adoption service, as well as service to the child's father (if he so desires).

One such organization is Evangelical Child and Family Agency, located in Chicago and Wheaton, Illinois. In interviewing Eleanor Hill, a counselor at ECFA, I sensed a real love and compassion for the unmarried pregnant girl and any others involved. For thirty-one years ECFA has helped children and families during times of stress and hardship. During that time, the agency has placed approximately 1,590 children in Christian adoptive homes, has cared for over 2,050 children in foster homes, and has helped approximately 2,290 unmarried parents. (For further information on ECFA consult chapter twelve, "Society and the Single Parent.")

Because of the huge cost to society, however, many organizations are having to cut back or go out of business. (Booth Memorial Hospitals, for example, have for many years ministered to unmarried girls under the auspices of the

Salvation Army. The hospital in Grand Rapids, Michigan, has been closed, and the Chicago hospital is now in jeopardy financially and may have to close.) Babies born to teenagers in 1978 cost taxpayers $8 billion in medical and welfare costs. The city of Chicago has four separate high schools just for pregnant teenagers. The budget for 1980 was $1.7 million for an enrollment of 1,100 girls at a time—and there was a waiting list.

While many teenagers and adults today feel that personal liberty is accomplished only with complete sexual freedom, there are many others who pursue a different kind of freedom. They have chosen to abstain from sexual activity until marriage, to exercise self-control. An article entitled "The Case for Chastity," written by Dr. Charles E. Millard (*Resident and Staff Physician,* April 1976) stresses the need for a disciplined life. In it he said:

A physician should be able to counsel all members of a family. An area which seems to have been sadly neglected, however, is how to counsel and support the single, adolescent girl who has chosen to remain chaste. The author feels that many doctors seem unable to give cogent and forceful support to these young ladies' important decision.

Dr. Millard suggests six freedoms of chastity:

Freedom from unwanted pregnancy.
Freedom from possible complications that occur with the pill.
Freedom from venereal disease.
Freedom from the effects of losing procreative powers

in those who elect sterilization by operation and those sterilized by venereal disease.

Freedom from the potential complications of abortion.

Freedom from the sorrow that descends on the family when an unmarried daughter becomes pregnant.

In addition to these six freedoms, Dr. Millard offered three more arguments the counseling physician could offer his patient:

Recognition that no studies have shown that premarital sex improves marriage and/or marital sex.

Development of self-discipline through abstinence—a trait needed in every other aspect of everyday living.

Chastity is the least expensive method of birth control.

Dana, a sixteen-year-old San Francisco high school junior exemplifies Dr. Millard's freedom philosophy. She said, "A guy will say, 'Everybody is doing it. What's the matter with you?' You just tell him 'Well, if everybody's doing it, find someone else to do it with' " (*Newsweek,* September 1, 1980). Dana is free indeed!

Teenage pregnancy and parenting are potentially hazardous to the health of the individuals directly involved and the well-being of the larger society. The Christian church can help by modeling in its homes and various types of families a loving and open communication and responsible behavior on the part of each family member. It can also be there to help pick up the pieces when young parents' lives fall apart. The gospel in action calls for one-on-one involvement in broken lives. While Christian organizations are a partial answer, Christian laypersons working with social services or other neighborhood and community groups can offer role models and support to children and their parents and wise counsel and responsible life-styles to young people not yet prepared for single-parent responsibility.

And hope is brightest when it dawns from fears. . . .

SIR WALTER SCOTT

I Shall Be Glad

If I can put new hope within the heart
Of one who has lost hope,
If I can help a brother up
Some difficult long slope
That seems too steep for tired feet to go,
If I can help him climb
Into the light upon the hill's far crest,
I shall begrudge no time
Or strength that I can spend, for well I know
How great may be his need.
If I can help through any darkened hour,
I shall be glad indeed.

For I recall how often I have been
Distressed, distraught, dismayed,
And hands have reached to help, and voices called
That kept me unafraid.
If I can share this help that I have had,
God knows I shall be glad.

GRACE NOLL CROWELL
Poems of Inspiration and Courage

3
Facing the Truth Emotionally

For most, becoming a single parent may be like giving birth to a barbed wire fence—extremely painful. But it also may be the beginning of a new you, and the journey into which you have been thrust will include many positive experiences.

If someone had made the first statement to me on January 19, 1959, I would have heartily agreed. My reaction to the second remark would have been, "How utterly ridiculous!"

That blustery, icy day I became a mother for the fourth time—but I was also given the news that my husband had only two years to live. From that day on I was, in many respects, a single parent.

We had many happy experiences during our fifteen years of marriage. Two delightful red-haired daughters and one golden blond "Dennis the Menace" son added extra spice and zest to our very busy lives in the parsonage. Each child had been dedicated to God immediately, read to extensively, played with creatively, loved intensely, and diligently taught Scripture and music. Each role in both our home and church ministry was very important.

Even on a shoestring budget we were able to picnic, swim, ice-skate, travel, and camp together. Intertwined with these happy events were the usual illnesses, accidents, and problems, along with some others of a very serious nature. One such illness is particularly vivid in my mind. During the worst polio epidemic the United States had had (American doctors reported 57,879 cases of polio in 1952, the highest number ever recorded) I held my six-year-old daughter in my arms; she was running a temperature of near 105 degrees. The doctor's anxious words staggered me, "Susan has polio. Put her in isolation immediately." Hesitantly I left her in the hospital and started on my twenty-five-mile trip home, weeping and praying. God guided the car on the highway, for I did not see or hear anything as I drove. "God, she is yours." I wept, finally acknowledging, after a churning emotional struggle, that Susan really belonged to God. He loved her, too! Many people, in various parts of the country, prayed for Susan that night. Her high fever began to subside the next morning. Two tense weeks in isolation, followed by several months at home in therapy, brought Susan back to health and gave me new insight into handling crisis experiences. It also gave me renewed assurance that I could depend on God to help me through any problem that might arise in the future.

Suddenly now, on that cold January day, the future loomed up before me as doctors indicated that one day I would face the responsibility of raising four children alone. We were both stunned, as was the family.

The predicted two years passed; more days, months, and years followed until my husband was completely incapacitated. Actual death arrived in our home June 29, 1964. I still vividly recall that day.

I can now say it was not the end of life, but it was, in fact, the beginning of a new me. I took a giant step forward in the journey God had planned especially for me. This realization did not come in a day, week, or month. It takes time to deal with one's emotions, and each person's adjustment takes a different route—the journey will vary.

I wish I could tell you I did everything right; that I could give you six easy steps to follow as you struggle to survive this new singleness. I can't! But I can share some ideas that have emerged through heartbreaking experience—the study, reading, mistakes, counseling, and sharing with others who had passed this way. I can share with you how God made Himself real to me in this time of crisis.

Aloneness

I felt alone! Desperately alone! This feeling came, and still comes occasionally, when I am truly alone—walking down a crowded street, shopping in a busy store, attending a gala party, or living with my four children. Aloneness is probably the first emotion that those who have recently become single through death or divorce must deal with.

> Listen to me for a day—an hour—a moment!
> Lest I expire in my terrible wilderness, my
> lonely silence! O God, is there no one to listen?
>
> SENECA

In his book *The Becomers,* Keith Miller says, "In a recent discussion, psychiatrists Jean Rosenbaum, Natalie Shainers, and Antonio Wenkart agreed that poignant loneliness is the most dangerous and widespread illness in America today...." Chronic loneliness affects from 75 to 90 percent of all Americans according to Dr. Rosenbaum.

Keith Miller adds, "But strangely, the problem is almost worse for Christians. We are subtly trained that if we are really restless or lonely, it may be a reflection on the depth of our commitment. So we repress these feelings and are conscious only of a strange franticness, or even boredom, or lack of interest in Christianity—which also can produce guilt."

Connie's husband left her with two small children to raise. She held a fine position in a large organization, had a lovely home and beautiful children, but rejection brought loneliness. "After so many disappointments in life," she wrote, "I struggle to commit my life completely into God's hands. I feel it is the only way I'll ever be able to gain peace, contentment, and strength to go on. I'm so tired of the tremendous turmoil I've been feeling inside—of the fear that grips me when I think of facing the future *alone*."

One important reason why aloneness is a major problem for many divorced or widowed single parents is that they have not developed a happy, fulfilled life as single persons. Connie's unique personality, for instance, had not been allowed to evolve apart from that of her mate (or apart from that of her parents before marriage).

Connie knew the secret of successfully resolving her conflicts as she recognized her need to commit her life "completely into God's hands." But recognition and appropriation are two different matters. Appropriation requires time and comes as we mature in our relationship with God.

Time is a precious commodity to a newly single parent. To tell an individual whose insides have been ripped into tiny shreds, "Time will heal," is not really very comforting.

Focusing on "God is with you, even though you may not feel like it right now" is more helpful in an hour of crisis.

Anger

Being thrown into a single state produces reactions other than loneliness. Anger, for instance: anger toward God for taking our mate in death; anger toward a mate for divorcing us; anger toward self for the part we played in becoming an unmarried single parent.

Death is undoubtedly the most traumatic experience in our lifetime. It is completely irreversible, but divorce is also shattering. It is, in essence, the death of a relationship. Is it any wonder, then, that we often express aloneness, anger, depression, anxiety, and guilt? We may allow these feelings to grow and destroy us, or we can deal with them as they occur and we can learn.

Depression

Everyone feels depressed from time to time. Depression may be cyclical, involving highs and lows. We really don't always understand what brings on our depression. Physical problems, guilt feelings, or something someone has said may precipitate a period of depression. High-stress situations, such as death and divorce, often produce severe depression.

"I had hoped the continued feeling of being lost could be overcome," wrote Jim, after his wife's death. "My work is becoming more demanding, and the home situation is almost a second job. I just haven't got it all together. Probably the most noticeable thing to me is the feeling of not being efficient. I've never been depressed for long lengths of time before. The question What's the use? accompanies depression. There's just too much to do, and I've not sorted it all out yet. God has lifted me part way out of the pit of loneliness, and I can partially see the light at the end of the dark tunnel. When a person feels himself sinking into that whirlpool of despair, it seems that life will only get worse, never better. What a terrible feeling."

I could relate to what Jim was saying. There were times I felt as though I was on a treadmill and could not stop. Often I felt as if I were taking one step forward and going back two. My mental gears kept slipping. Life became a constant whirl of paying bills, getting the car to the garage for tune-up or repair, cleaning house, working forty hours a week, disciplining children, resolving conflicts, and a hundred nitty-gritty details that were often overwhelming. As a single parent I had to assume all the responsibilities I had as a mother, plus all the things Father had done when he was well and strong.

Somewhere along the line life began to take on shape and form again. After much readjustment and organization, life became tolerable and finally worthwhile, meaningful, and even happy. (Loneliness, depression, anger, and high-stress situations will be dealt with in more detail in chapter six, "The Crisis Cycle.")

Special Days

Holidays, birthdays, and anniversaries are especially difficult for those left alone through death or divorce. But special days may bring problems to the unmarried parent or single adoptive parent as well. Christmas seems to trigger a special type of depression. To begin with, we naturally dread going through this season alone. Besides, it often fails to meet expectations that we have built up over a number of weeks. Another reason may be that buying gifts seems meaningless now that our special one has gone; and finally, we are often left with depressing bills to pay.

"Six months have elapsed since my wife's death," Joe quietly confided. "In September we would have had our twenty-fifth wedding anniversary. Each of these special times accentuates her absence. Last Thanksgiving, for instance, was the last day she really felt good and acted her natural self. I really don't look forward to Christmas this year."

One Valentine's Day I was invited to a party with several couples. I had been to many gatherings with "just couples" after my husband's death. But for some reason this party brought a lump in my throat and an empty feeling in the pit of my stomach. It would have been very easy to leave the party and go home, feeling "poor me." Pondering my feelings I realized these were my dear friends. I loved them, and they loved me. I hadn't been invited because they felt sorry for me. They wanted me to be with them. Why should I ruin my evening and theirs by feeling sorry for myself? It's good to be wanted and included.

Everyone responds to crisis: men, women, and children—rich or poor, educated or uneducated, young or old—no one is exempt! Some become angry, others depressed, and still others isolate themselves to a lonely existence.

> Acknowledge your true feelings: loneliness, anger, guilt, depression, others.
> Recognize *aloneness* as the first feeling most newly single parents experience.

Realize that it takes *time* to heal.

Be prepared for special days that may be difficult to face. Plan ahead to keep from being alone.

Begin to develop your own unique personality—this is God's will for you. Study: Psalm 139; Isaiah 43:1–4, 7; Philippians 2:1–18.

Learn more about God and how He helps people through crisis experiences. Study: 2 Chronicles 20: 1–12; Acts 7:1–50.

Believe that the Bible is true. Memorize the following passages to help you through your personal crisis: Psalm 23; Joshua 1:9; Hebrews 13:5.

Read to gain understanding of yourself, your problems, and God.

Suggested Reading

Bachmann, Charles C. *Ministering to the Grief Sufferer.* Englewood Cliffs, N.J.: Prentice-Hall, 1964.

Brown, Velma Darbo. *After Weeping, a Song.* Nashville: Broadman, 1980.

Caine, Lynn. *Widow.* New York: Bantam Books, 1975.

Champagne, Marion. *Facing Life Alone.* Indianapolis: Bobbs-Merrill, 1964.

Chavez, Patricia, and Cartland, Clif. *Picking up the Pieces.* Nashville, Thomas Nelson, 1979.

Crook, Roger H. *An Open Book to the Christian Divorcée.* Nashville: Broadman, 1974.

Ellison, Craig W. *Loneliness: The Search for Intimacy.* New York: Christian Herald, 1980.

Gorer, Geoffrey. *Death, Grief, and Mourning.* ed., Robert Kastenbaum. New York: Doubleday, 1977.

Haggai, John E. *How to Win Over Loneliness.* Nashville: Thomas Nelson, 1979.

Hulme, William E. *Creative Loneliness.* Minneapolis: Augsburg, 1977.

Jackson, Edgar N. *You and Your Grief.* New York: Hawthorn Books, 1961.

Johnson, James. *Loneliness Is Not Forever.* Chicago: Moody Press, 1979.

Kooiman, Gladys. *When Death Takes a Father.* Grand Rapids: Baker Book House, 1968.

Lockyer, Herbert. *How to Find Comfort in the Bible.* Waco, Texas: Word Books, 1977.

Lyman, Howard B. *Single Again.* New York: David McKay, 1971.

Westberg, Granger E. *Good Grief.* Philadelphia: Fortress Press, 1962.

The child's grief throbs against its little
heart as heavily as the man's sorrow. . . .

E. H. CHAPIN

4
Children Suffer, Too!

"How can you believe God is a God of love when He allowed my dad to suffer and die?" cried my teenage son as he ran down the stairs. "I prayed for him every day, and look what happened."

Tears flowed freely down my cheeks, too, as I agonized with Stan in his hour of anger and grief. My insides were torn up as I listened to my child cry out against God—my God!—whom I had trusted, depended upon, believed in since childhood. This was the God of my husband's faith also. Seeing his body deteriorate into nothing did not cause him to deny that God was his God and a God of love, at that.

Had we, or others, failed to communicate this deep love and faith to Stan? As lovingly as possible I said, "Stan, I'm sorry you are angry with God. I must tell you I have no ill feeling toward Him. I could not have survived the long years without God. He has met our needs, provided a home, food, clothing, good job, loving family, and healthy bodies and minds. He gave strength, courage, and intelligence to see us through this crisis. I love God very much, Stan. I don't understand the reason for Dad's illness and death, but I can certainly understand how you feel."

Death, divorce, and desertion call for a time of grief. Children, too, respond by becoming angry, depressed, or lonely.

Had I been more aware, before death arrived in our home, of how deeply children are affected by crisis, my relationship with them and theirs with me would have been smoother. The readjustment process would also have involved less time.

After going through the same long years of strain and struggle that I had, my four children now felt a new freedom. Their leader, though bedridden, was gone. Gone, forever! Shortly after the funeral, when relatives and friends returned to their own homes, we faced the lonely truth. The sooner we begin to establish a new way of life—new routines—the better, I reasoned; so we quickly got rid of wheelchair, medicine, special equipment, and clothing. This did not, however, make it any easier. It was extremely difficult to enter a deathly quiet house.

For many months prior to my husband's death someone was at home twenty-four hours a day. Sounds, smells, and sights may be pleasant and can certainly be warm and comforting. Now the luscious aroma of roast beef flavored with onion soup did not permeate the air as we opened the door; familiar voices, bickering over the Detroit Tiger baseball game on television, were no longer heard, and the happy sound from the piano no longer implied Welcome Home! To top it off, "live bodies" were not there to personally greet us.

In all honesty, our home became more like a funeral parlor after Father's death than before. The quietness and freedom were absolutely devastating.

Out of sheer necessity I had been a "mother figure," rushing about, going to work, paying bills, bringing home food, and keeping peace in the midst of confusion. Even though I did most of the work, to the children I was not the *leader* of our home. Adjusting to me in my new role was difficult for them. My husband and I should have better prepared them to accept me as head of the house. What a power-packed, explosive bunch to raise alone—ages five, eleven, fifteen, and seventeen. I often felt the situation was hopeless. Our older daughter longed for a man's love to replace the love her father had given her. Son Stan began to get into mischief at home, school, church, and in society in general. He seemed to be venting his pent-up anger against God, the family, and the rest of the world. David became fearful. Sharon seemingly adjusted well, but inside she felt that I was never there when she needed me.

How could I possibly help my children adjust to a new way of life when I was exhausted from five long years of my husband's illness? There were times when I felt completely inadequate for the task. As I began to recognize the frightening feeling of abandonment that the children felt and some of my own inadequacies, I realized this was just the kind of situation God used to prove His tremendous power and ability to meet every need. My relationship with the children, as individuals and as a family group, slowly began to improve. For five years our lives had been devoted to a united effort to make husband and father as comfortable as possible. Oh, yes, we had many activities as individuals, but the main thrust of our concerted effort was toward husband and father. It would take time and patience to adjust to a new style of living.

Children living with a single parent may have many questions, often unspoken ones. They may think: *One member of my family has disappeared; will the other member leave me, too?* or, *Who will protect and care for me now that my dad is gone?* or, *I wonder who and where my "real" father is? Why was I adopted? Didn't my parents love me? I wonder why I only have a mother and why she never married.* These questions are legitimate and need answering, to give a child assurance that someone will continue to care for him.

I faced some of these questions myself. David, our youngest, became very fearful. I, too, had fears that needed to be dealt with—such as driving long distances on freeways and through mountains. I planned a trip to help me overcome my fears. Loading the children into the car, I started out from our home in Michigan and drove five hundred miles to a state park in New York. We had planned to reach the park by early evening. Apparently my tiredness and fears came across loud and clear to David. He said over and over, "Mother, do you think we'll make it?" or, "I'm afraid." After what seemed like dozens of rest-room stops, tons of pop, and nit-picking among the children, we arrived at 9:00 P.M.—just as the park office was ready to close. How good it was to unload, safe and sound and tired, in the beautiful mountains. This was the beginning of some positive steps for the entire family, even though life looked rather negative at times.

Had I been better prepared to cope with just the driving experience alone, David would undoubtedly have been less tense. But more important, had I felt better about myself as a person, the children would have experienced less anxiety also.

Sigmund Freud is said to have made the statement: "Being a parent is an impossible profession under even the best of circumstances."

As Christians we look at parenthood more positively than this, but Freud was right, parenthood is a big job. But when one becomes a single, through circumstances or by choice, children may very well react with fears or other behavior not previously evidenced. One child may withdraw, another may become disobedient, yet another critical, and a fourth might appear totally accepting of the crisis, yet be seething inside over the inequities life seems to heap on him.

Given the opportunity, teenagers will express their uncertainties. "One of my biggest problems now," said Katie, "is that I have no family relationship because I have no family left—both mother and father are dead. I'm going through a time when I need guidance very much; and also I need close relationships with people, the kind which I no longer can have from a family. I often wonder about security and my own capability for handling myself."

Bonnie recognized the important role death had played in her home as she related to me, "When I was eight my life was changed drastically by the tragic death of my mother. Death is very confusing to a child, and it was difficult for me to comprehend that I would never see my mother again."

"I was extremely close to my father and miss him greatly, as we used to do many things together," John quietly told me. "Most of all I miss his crazy sense of humor and can't get used to not being teased very much anymore. I loved him deeply, and it was a tremendous shock to me when he died."

"My homelife is quite difficult to explain," Rosalie confided. "My mother died when I was ten years old, so my father and I moved in with my married sister and her four children. My father later remarried, and I was given the choice of living with my sister or my father, his wife, and her three children. I chose to live with my sister because I was very uneasy about moving in with a strange family and sharing my father. I also felt my mother would have wanted me to live with my sister."

Cindy began to tell me her tragic story by saying, "My father came to tell me he was divorcing my mother and marrying another woman. For the first time in my life my father held me and told me he loved me. That moment is very precious to me now. He left that day—gone forever. I was completely torn apart. I didn't talk to anyone, and I didn't do anything. I nearly failed all my classes in school. The worst of it all was that I could not pray. I didn't know why then; I don't know why now, but it was a terrible feeling. I was hurt, lonely, frightened, and confused. Finally, after several months God began to heal the wound, and I found relief."

Marie never knew her father—nor the circumstances surrounding her birth. She lived with her mother, various relatives, and baby-sitters, until the age of three (during which time her mother entertained many boyfriends). Her mother then left her with a family who wanted to adopt her. She stayed with this loving and attentive family for several months, but then her mother came to take her back. Her mother was married to one man for nine years—he didn't care about Marie—and was then divorced. From this time on Marie was exposed to many boyfriends and "fathers"— all of whose presence she now refused to acknowledge. Each time her mother started with a new husband or wanted to move to a new town she asked Marie if she liked the man, and Marie always said yes. In fact, she knew that whether or not she liked the man, it would make no difference. She was moved around from state to state and from city to city, from ages eleven to eighteen, never having had a stable homelife (mother was working, too) and existing largely on chocolate cake and Coke.

Marie emerged from a shy childhood as a shy, withdrawn adult, afraid of strange situations, new people, and forming close relationships. It was only recently (at the age of forty) that she began to open up to anyone—family or friend—about any personal feelings, needs, desires, or wants. Instead, she had withdrawn to the comfort of a bottle of alcohol, spending most nights drinking herself to sleep.

Through the counsel and love of a good friend she is now making steady progress toward control of her drinking; she is attending college and seeking to establish a more responsible and fulfilling life.

A year after his father's death, my son Stan wrote an eighth-grade English paper in which he expressed some of his intense feelings.

I feel evil is done because of emotions. Periods when one is sad and rather angry cause people to do things that may seem insane. I don't believe that insanity has anything to do with evil. Once again I say, evil comes from having sad, angry feelings. These feelings can come from many sources. A lot of them may come from losing a member of the family, or a close relative. These feelings may also be affected by the loss of a job or the loss of a lot of money. When a boy loses a girl he has liked for a long time he sometimes becomes very angry. This world is an evil place, and there are people who are probably glad to die and get out of it.

David, our youngest, also expressed his feelings about grief when he wrote a poem in sixth grade and called it "Human Misery."

> It's like losing in sports,
> Or a relative dies,
> Like totaling a brand new car,
> Maybe your ceiling caves in.

As a family we had experienced everything David mentioned except totaling a brand new car. He understood crisis—truly human misery.

Home environment before and after a crisis, circumstances of the crisis, and the emotional characteristics of the remaining parent are determining factors in the child's adjustment after a crisis experience.

Authors Roy B. Zuck and Gene A. Getz, in *Christian Youth—An In-Depth Study,* reported on 3,000 teenagers. Their morals, values, doubts, religious practices, social characteristics, and evaluations of themselves and their families and churches were studied. Death, divorce, and unstable homes appear to be responsible for many problems teenagers encounter:

Teens from broken homes (27.1%) and nonchristian homes (26.2%) expressed the greatest concern over their schoolwork. This observation, of course, compares favorably with psychological studies which have pointed to a cause-effect relationship between feelings of anxiety and the ability to learn. It is assumed from this observation that evangelical young people who come from broken homes or homes that are not unified religiously and socially may be subject to certain frustrations and conflicts which in turn detrimentally affect their ability to concentrate and to apply themselves academically.

Loneliness and discouragement were also higher among youths from broken homes.

[In three categories, academic ability, personal adequacy, and social relationships] family disunity consistently appears as a factor showing important differences. On every item related to social concern, teens with separated or divorced parents expressed more dissatisfaction.

Concern over inadequacy and excessiveness in family harmony and parent-teen relationships is slightly higher among youths from broken homes.

Teens from broken homes stated that interest in spiritual things, closeness in the family, and parental interest in them personally were lacking; and they also indicated, more than other teens, that their parents leave them too much on their own.

As might be expected, the greatest differences related to future happiness in marriage. Apparently, the Christian youth who had observed the lack of marital unity in their own homes tended to wonder if they themselves would enjoy happiness in marriage. Accordingly, the one item with the greatest differential was assurance that they would marry someone with whom genuine happiness could be shared.

Teens in families that were ruptured by parental separation or divorce were less aware of God's nearness and more disturbed over the little time they spend in studying the Bible. These teens also showed greater concern over their academic problems, family unity, moral conduct on dates, future happiness in marriage; they also had more questions about evangelical doctrines.

The problems we experienced in our family resulted largely from the length and seriousness of my husband's illness. It was also very difficult for the children to understand how God could be a God of love and yet allow their father to suffer for so many years, and then to die.

Working through some of the very real problems we faced, I discovered that we had been too legalistic, for one thing. Stan, for example, had not been allowed to play Little League baseball—an excellent, legitimate outlet for an energetic young man. Encouraging him to become actively engaged in sports, I also became an enthusiastic spectator. It was a delight to watch him excel in football, baseball, basketball, and track.

One gets beyond *What will people say?* when children have problems. That is irrelevant. I began, rather, to evaluate what I could have done better in order to help the other children. Going to the depths of each problem I asked myself, *How can I reach the innermost being of this troubled child and help him begin to build a new life?* My thoughts, words, and actions were analyzed in light of how they would be interpreted by my children. How can I, by my life, help them know that God loves them? that I love them? How can I show deep love without spoiling, compromising? Of course, I had to begin by loving sincerely, deeply, and un-selfishly—loving in spite of failure. Always saying: "Let's try again. We'll do better next time." Being honest: "I can't condone the wrong, but I love you deeply. I'm always by your side to help—not always physically—but I'm there be-cause I'm praying for you constantly. The principles we've talked about will return in time of need—when temptation strikes too close."

Almost every night became a counseling session with my older son—although he did not realize it. "How about a rubdown, Mom?" he would say after a busy, tiring day of school and sports activities. My answer almost without ex-ception was yes because this was a marvelous time for com-munication, sharing the day's joys and sorrows, and work-ing through problems. There was little prying, just talking and quietly sharing. Here is a wonderful method to get an extremely active, busy, domineering young man to become "clay," soft clay, capable of being molded into something fine. Many nights I got out of bed, weary after working all day. I did not resent this intrusion. Not only were these times valuable to Stan, but to me, for they gave me an in-sight into a very complicated young man. We constantly worked on values and standards, to help him learn to make good judgments and decisions.

Life need not be a tragedy for young children, teenagers, and young adults, during or after a crisis. However, they will need guidance and security at this time because they feel torn apart. There may be difficulties academically, socially, spiritually, and emotionally. Children, in grief, will express their emotions in differing ways. Loneliness and sadness can be expected. There may be anger toward self or others or God—or a turning against God. Some become fearful; others may withdraw, resort to alcohol or drugs. Decisions and choices may be difficult for children to make during this period. Divorce may bring about hurt, fright, confusion, and frustration. Some children express insecurity in "sharing" a parent with a new family.

Recognizing that children go through a grief process, just as you do, you can look for creative ways to help them through this crisis period.

> Ask yourself honest questions; then search for answers to meet your family's needs.
>
> Seek counseling for yourself and your children. Getting help is sensible.
>
> Realize the importance of the home environment and look for positive ways to improve it.
>
> Seek creative ways to meet your children's needs.
>
> Participation in sports and other activities can be encouraged.
>
> Meet their physical needs by loving them (a hug, kiss, or pat), playing with them, or helping them relax (rubdown).
>
> Children who are sad need some humor in the home.
>
> Pray for and with your children. Teach them that they may trust God.
>
> Study John 11 to help you understand the emotional needs of others and how Christ met these needs in the people to whom He ministered.

Suggested Reading

Arnstein, Helene S. *What to Tell Your Child.* Indianapolis: Bobbs-Merrill, 1962.

Ewing, Kathryn. *A Private Matter.* New York: Harcourt, Brace Jovanovich, 1975.

Gardner, Richard A. *Boys and Girls Book About Divorce.* New York: Bantam Books, 1971.

Grollman, Earl A., ed. *Explaining Death to Children.* Boston: Beacon Press, 1969.

Grollman, Earl A. *Talking About Death.* Boston: Beacon Press, 1972.

Lexau, Joan M. *Me Day.* New York: Dial Press, 1971.

Mann, Peggy. *My Dad Lives in a Downtown Hotel.* New York: Doubleday, 1973.

Mazer, Norma. *I, Trissy.* New York: Delacorte Press, 1971.

Pevsner, Stella. *A Smart Kid Like You.* New York: Seabury Press, 1974.

Wotherspoon, Lee. *Dear Kids.* Newton, N.H.: Dear Kids Pubs., 1973.

Troubles of Childhood

"Ah, my child, you will have real troubles to fret about by-and-by," is the consolation we have almost all of us had administered to us in our childhood, and have repeated to other children since we have grown up. We have all of us sobbed so piteously, standing with tiny bare legs above our socks, when we lost sight of our mother or nurse in some strange place; but we can no longer recall the poignancy of that moment and weep over it, as we do over the remembered sufferings of five or ten years ago. Every one of those keen moments has left its trace, and lives in us still, but such traces have blent themselves irrecoverably with the firmer texture of our youth and manhood; and so it comes that we can look on at the troubles of our children with a smiling disbelief in the reality of their pain. . . . Surely, if we could recall that early bitterness, and the dim guesses, the strangely perspectiveless conception of life that gave the bitterness its intensity, we should not pooh-pooh the griefs of our children.

GEORGE ELIOT
Mill on the Floss

5
Emotionally Damaged Children

Anyone who has lost one of his parents as a child is three times more likely to experience some form of emotional breakdown in later life than one who has kept them both, one study reports. As this child grows into adulthood and faces a crisis he may remember his earlier loss and feel angry toward a parent for "deserting him." However, he also feels guilty for having such terrible resentments toward the parent.

Susie Low self-concept and feelings of inadequacy plagued Susie through life. She came from a society where the need was always greater than the supply. Depression is no respecter of persons—rich or poor, young or old, scholarly or uneducated. All are susceptible and vulnerable to this miserable state of mind.

Susie's dad had deserted the family when the children were very young. Her mother valiantly struggled to keep the family together, but there never seemed to be quite enough of anything to go around. They lived many places, none really quite adequate for a growing family. The mother knew little about self-esteem, so she was unable to teach her children how to live successfully in this less than desirable environment. After Susie and others in the family came into a loving relationship with God, the future appeared somewhat brighter. A young man entered the picture, and wedding bells rang for this happy couple. They looked forward to a lifetime of love.

The lack of confidence, inner conflicts, and depression she had grown up with began to surround Susie again, shortly after her marriage. As babies arrived, especially after the birth of a son, deep depression and a sense of futility set in. The unexpressed anger she felt toward her father for deserting the family was now being expressed in anger toward her husband and son. She also hated herself and felt very guilty for having such terrible resentments toward the men in her life. Many counseling sessions followed. At times she seemed to make good progress; on other occasions she plunged into deep despair. Just when hope for recovery loomed brightly on the horizon, her heartbroken husband came home one day to find that Susie had taken her own life in a final act of desperation.

Sherri   Sherri, a beautiful girl, was a daughter of divorce. She confided that her mother had been too permissive; her father was an authoritarian. Her mother had been involved in many "affairs," and Sherri simply could not trust her. She felt physically divided—her left side belonging to her father and her right side to her mother. In her own words, "I had a dual personality and behaved one way with my mother, another with my father." Because her mother hated all forms of housework, Sherri was forced to do much of it. In doing so, she felt like the mother of the home. Though she was for all practical purposes the "mother," she had no control over her mother's unacceptable behavior. These circumstances caused Sherri much confusion, and as a result of years of such trauma, she experienced some unusual behavior herself. She felt great relief when she finally moved in with her father, even though he was too strict for a time. Sherri prefers the authority of her father, administered with love, to the permissiveness of her mother, with little love. She is becoming a mature, stable person after many struggling years. Fortunately, Sherri has had the help of Christian counselors and the love of relatives and friends.

Mike Less secure masculine identity, more dependent behavior, decreased school performance, poorer peer-group relationships, and increased incidence of emotional illness are cited as possible consequences to boys because of a father's absence in the home.

Mike's family had traveled and lived in many parts of the world. Anyone looking on would have said, "They have a good life!" But prestige, travel, and money are not necessarily ingredients with which to build a stable home environment.

For many years Mike's dad had enjoyed the company of several female companions other than his wife. Finally obtaining a divorce, he soon remarried, leaving his family shattered.

Mike was crushed, angry, and confused. "How could my dad do this to me? I trusted him," he questioned. Mike retreated into a little world all his own and refused to go to school or be with other young people. He finally became paranoid, believing someone was out to kill him.

Fortunately, a loving mother helped him through this traumatic period of life. Wise counselors assured him he was not responsible for his father's problems, and they guided him in establishing a firm relationship with his Heavenly Father, God. He now realizes how much God loves him and that God will never fail him. God can be trusted!

Jerry Jerry, seventeen, was hostile! There was no doubt about it. He seemed to be in constant trouble everywhere he went, including trouble with the law. His dad had died when Jerry was quite small. Now his mother was in the hospital, desperately ill. In a moment of anger and frustration he lashed out at her, "I wish you would die." What he was really saying was, "Please, Mother, don't you leave me, too." The hurt of separation from a loved one goes deeper than we realize, and only in such an outburst can we really "hear" what Jerry is saying.

Bill "The emotional climate of the child's home life is probably the most important factor in the development of delinquent behavior," according to Dr. Clyde M. Narramore (*Encyclopedia of Psychological Problems*). "Glueck and Glueck, in a comparison of 500 pairs of juvenile delinquents, found a very high percent of the delinquents came from homes broken by separation, divorce, death, or prolonged absence of a parent."

Bill was a handsome, polite, intelligent teenager. His home was anything but stable. His dad drank heavily, had a terrible temper, and was unfaithful to Bill's mother. She finally gave up in despair, believing there was no hope for her marriage.

After the divorce became final, Bill and his mother moved in with his grandparents. His mother was extremely involved in her work and in earning money to support herself and her son. She had little time for Bill, and his grandparents had no control over him.

One night Bill became drunk and seriously injured another young man. After this tragic experience, he was very fearful of being sent to prison. Friends of the family who knew Bill realized his unstable homelife was the major reason for his problems and urged the judge not to resort to such harsh measures as prison. Bill had a great deal of potential. What he needed most of all was love, attention, and supervision.

The judge ruled that Bill and his family were to have extensive counseling. Fortunately, Bill responded to the counseling and eventually went into the service, where he became efficient and capable in the field of electronics.

Many parents do not recognize the relationship between the crisis experience and their child's behavior. Once the cause of the behavior problem has been established, it becomes easier to work toward a solution.

Girls need the influence of a woman, and boys need male influence after losing a parent. Because so few people are aware of the tremendous need in the lives of children with only one parent, single parents, themselves, may be excellent substitutes. The time spent is not only valuable to the children, but to the substitute parent as well—it can be both a learning and a healing experience.

Personally, I found it very easy to stop and pick up one more child to take to a ball game, simple to put another plate on the table for dinner, and gratifying to change the linen for an overnight guest.

Youth workers, camp counselors, ministers, teachers, friends, and neighbors also need to be aware of the needs of young people left without parents. A man could play an important role by taking a young boy fishing or on a weekend camping trip.

My own son helped me realize how much he needed an older male model when he said to me, "Mom, I really appreciate your faithfulness in attending all my ball games and backing me up in sports, but it just isn't quite the same as having a dad there. I hope you understand what I'm trying to say." I understood completely and appreciated his honesty. It was good that he was able to share his feelings with me.

Most children and young people respond very positively to any love and kindness shown them. It's up to us, as single parents, to do everything we can to lessen the grief and anxiety that the loss of a parent brings.

We may be products of the past, but we need not be prisoners of the past. With counseling and guidance we can help ourselves and our children to live fulfilled lives.

> Begin to establish a stable home so that the chance of emotional problems occurring will be lessened.
>
> Recognize that children want and need love, attention, and supervision.
>
> Where differences of opinion have occurred (too permissive versus too authoritarian) attempt to become more balanced. Settle this equitably so that your child will not be frustrated.
>
> Determine the cause of behavior problems. Look for the real meaning of emotional outbursts. Realize that children, in their anger, do not always mean what they say.

Seek counseling from a reputable Christian psychologist, psychiatrist, or minister.

Begin to read books that will help you to develop a good self-concept, learn who you are, and why you do things the way you do.

Read books that may help in learning to balance discipline and love.

Suggested Reading

Dobson, James. *Dare to Discipline.* Wheaton, Ill.: Tyndale House, 1970.

———. *The Strong-Willed Child.* Wheaton, Ill.: Tyndale House, 1978.

LaHaye, Tim. *Spirit-Controlled Temperament.* Wheaton, Ill.: Tyndale House, 1966.

———. *Transformed Temperaments.* Wheaton, Ill.: Tyndale House.

Narramore, S. Bruce. *Help! I'm a Parent* (with manual *A Guide to Child Rearing*). Grand Rapids: Zondervan, 1972.

———. *An Ounce of Prevention.* Grand Rapids: Zondervan, 1973.

Narramore, Clyde M. *Understanding Your Children.* New York: Pyramid Pubs., 1969.

But he knoweth the way that I take: when he hath tried me, I shall come forth as gold.

Job 23:10

There is nothing—no circumstance, no trouble, no testing—that can ever touch me until, first of all, it has gone past God and past Christ, right through to me. If it has come that far, it has come with a great purpose, which I may not understand at the moment; but as I refuse to become panicky, as I lift my eyes up to Him and accept it as coming from the throne of God for some great purpose of blessing to my own heart, no sorrow will ever disturb me, no trial will ever disarm me, no circumstance will cause me to fret, for I shall rest in the joy of what my Lord is. That is the rest of victory.

ALAN REDPATH
Victorious Christian Living

6
The Crisis Cycle

"Life begins at forty" is an old adage, and to a certain degree I would have to say that, though life did not actually begin at forty for me, it certainly took a sharp turn; for it was at this age that my husband died, and I had to decide what to do with the remainder of my life. A new and different style of living evolved. It came, however, after years of preparation—"forty years of wandering," so to speak. Without these years of preparation I could not have faced the challenges and difficulties that were yet before me.

You, too, have been in preparation for the time of crisis you are going through. Maybe you haven't had time to sit down and evaluate what has happened and where you are going—or maybe you haven't wanted to! But evaluation is important and helpful in beginning a new life-style. Granted, evaluation often hurts, especially when change needs to take place in one's life. Theodore Irwin discusses what a crisis means in a Public Affairs Pamphlet *How to Cope With Crises* (No. 464).

Harvard psychiatrist Dr. Gerald Caplan defines a personal crisis as a critical transition point or as a disruption of a person's "steady state" of existence by a disturbing situation. Precisely, a crisis in this sense is an *emotional* state, the reaction of an individual or a family to the hazardous event—not the event or situation itself. This state affects such vital goals as life, security, and affectional ties. During this period the victim is thrown off balance. For him, the crisis represents a turning point for better or worse, depending on the decisions he makes. If he copes effectively, he is likely to strengthen his potential for a rewarding life. Thus, one characteristic of a crisis—which most of us may not realize—is the chance it presents for enriching our personality. A crisis may then be viewed as a catalyst that shakes up old habits and can help us chart new ways.

Jeanette and Ralph are examples of people whose lives were not enriched by crisis situations. Jeanette, an attractive wife, mother, and community-minded woman, was found dead in her car of carbon monoxide poisoning. She could not cope with the shattering news that her husband was leaving her for another woman. Ralph's wife died suddenly and left him feeling very depressed. He became a loner, critical, and caustic. As time passed, he was plagued by migraine headaches and high blood pressure.

In his book *Helplessness,* Dr. Martin Seligman of the University of Pennsylvania supports the view that:

Helplessness seems to make people more vulnerable to the pathogens, some deadly, that are always around us. When one of our parents dies (or when our own spouse dies), we must be particularly careful. I suggest complete bi-monthly physical checkups during the first year following the loss. It seems to me wise to adopt this procedure following *any* major life change.

Psychiatrist Thomas Holmes and physiologist Minoru Masuda of the University of Washington School of Medicine, Seattle, propose a scale to help predict stress-related illness. They found that changes in a person's life, whether good or bad, could have a stressful effect and lead to disease. For most people, the death of a spouse, divorce, and separation were all high on the scale as events that produced stress; but marriage, a job change, buying a house, or receiving an award were also often traumatic. Whether good or bad, life changes appear "to have relevance to the causation of disease, its time of onset, and its severity," says Dr. Holmes.

It's very important to recognize that even a happy event like adoption may be stressful. For example, changes in living conditions; revision of personal habits; change in recreation, church, and social activities; change in sleeping and eating habits could all occur. Pregnancy for the unmarried will bring distress; for the married, joy!

Point values were assigned to various events in a person's life, depending on how often, and in what proportion, they accompanied an illness. In a pilot study 93 percent of all major illnesses were associated with a clustering of life changes whose value totaled at least 150 points annually. Not every major life change or crisis produced illness, but several of them together could add up to do so. Of persons with life changes totaling 150–199 points, 37 percent had an illness. When changes totaled 200–299, it was 51 percent; over 300 points, 79 percent became ill. Life events that appear to affect our health, with the point values assigned to these events, are listed here:

Life Event	Value
Death of spouse	100
Divorce	73
Marital separation	65
Jail term	63
Death of close family member	63
Personal injury or illness	53
Marriage	50
Fired at work	47
Marital reconciliation	45
Retirement	45
Change in health of family member	44
Pregnancy	40
Sexual difficulties	39
Gain of new family member	39
Business readjustment	39
Change in financial state	38
Death of close friend	37
Change to different line of work	36
Change in number of arguments with spouse	35
Mortgage over $10,000	31
Foreclosure of mortgage or loan	30
Change in responsibilities at work	29
Son or daughter leaving home	29
Trouble with in-laws	29
Outstanding personal achievement	28
Wife begins or stops work	26
Begin or end school	26
Change in living conditions	25
Revision of personal habits	24
Trouble with boss	23

Change in work hours or conditions	20
Change in schools	20
Change in recreation	19
Change in church activities	19
Change in social activities	18
Mortgage or loan less than $10,000	17
Change in sleeping habits	16
Change in number of family get-togethers	15
Change in eating habits	15
Vacation	13
Christmas	12
Minor violations of the law	11

How many of these changes or events are happening, or have happened, to you within the past few months? Does this give you an indication as to why you suffer from head-aches, stomachaches, and backaches (or possibly more severe illnesses) from time to time?

When we experience crises, the rest of the world appears to be moving normally around us. We feel anesthetized and do not really know what we, or others, are doing. We are in shock! Adjustment to any crisis experience is a long process—different for each individual.

For example, family members and patients experience a variety of reactions and emotions after learning of a forthcoming death. According to sociologists, family members follow a course of: disbelief, numbness, mourning, trial-and-error adjustment, renewal of routine, and finally recovery. Elisabeth Kübler-Ross in her book *On Death and Dying* notes that the patient himself passes through specific stages in life's last journey:

1. Denial—no, not me!
2. Anger—why me?
3. Bargaining—a campaign, often undetectable, to somehow stay execution of sentence.
4. Depression—the patient is weighing the fearful price of death, preparing himself to accept the loss of everything and of everyone he loves.
5. Acceptance—I am now ready and no longer afraid.

These stages are marked on The Crisis Cycle diagram as they are similar to the stages and reactions which may be experienced in any adverse life change. This defines what happens to persons going through crises, ranging from death or divorce to trouble with children or work upsets.

The Crisis Cycle

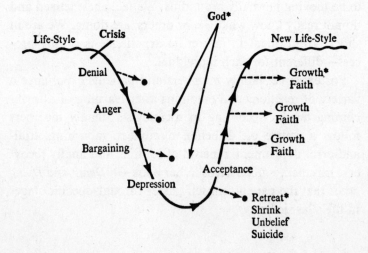

The human being passes through a variety of life-styles. For example, after graduating from college, a man may accept a position with a prominent organization, marry, and have children. His life-style is smooth and successful for several years. One day his boss says, "Because of extensive reorganization within our corporation, your job is being phased out." He goes home stunned. His wife and children respond to his stress over the crisis experience. Anxiety and fear turn into anger and depression—toward himself, the organization, and his family. Eventually, his wife becomes critical because he lost his job, and they no longer enjoy the good life. Finally, he gives up in despair, leaving his wife and children. As a result, a new life-style emerges for every member of the family as father and mother go their separate ways.

In her book *On Death and Dying* Elisabeth Kübler-Ross goes carefully through each step of the dying process.

First Stage: Denial "No, not me—it cannot be true" is the first reaction. I remember vividly when the doctor first told us that my husband probably had no more than two years to live. Our response was denial, "It can't be true." We said to ourselves and to each other, "It won't happen! It just can't happen! God wouldn't let this happen to us after we've faithfully served Him."

Second Stage: Anger "Why me?" usually follows the denial stage. A friend who had been a widow for two years attended a crisis-intervention meeting. Someone questioned her, "Why are you angry over your husband's death?" The widow quickly and angrily replied, "I am not angry. Why do you say that?" After arriving home she pondered her friend's statement and recognized that she really was angry. Admitting her anger helped her move on to the next stage.

Third Stage: Bargaining   After dealing with anger, an individual may think that if he talks nicely or bargains with God, God's decision may be changed. I knew of two young mothers who bargained with God—each for the same thing. They each asked God to allow them to live to care for their children. One faced death from tuberculosis—the other from cancer. God answered their prayers differently. The mother who asked in 1928 is alive today at eighty-two. The mother who asked in 1972, at thirty-four years of age, died of metastatic carcinoma, leaving five children who were under thirteen years of age.

Bargaining is often used when divorce is involved. For example, an individual may say, "I promise I won't step out on you again if you will give me another chance."

Fourth Stage: Depression   This stage is the most difficult, and the depressed individual needs careful attention. In his book *Helplessness,* Martin Seligman says: "The label 'depression' applies to passive individuals who believe they cannot do anything to relieve their suffering, who become depressed when they lose an important source of nurture—the perfect case for learned helplessness to model; but it also applies to agitated patients who make many active responses, and who become depressed with no obvious external cause."

According to the Crisis Cycle diagram, depression may involve: retreat, shrinking or withdrawal, unbelief, suicide. The line indicates that an individual going from one lifestyle to another descends into a valley which may be compared to the "valley of the shadow of death," which is mentioned in the Twenty-third Psalm. The Psalm says further that we do not walk through this valley alone, nor need we fear evil, for God is with us. The Christian can be assured that he is never alone: "The Lord is my shepherd; I shall not want." As indicated by the arrows on the Crisis Cycle diagram, God is with us during each stage of life's journey.

Fifth Stage: Acceptance   "If a patient has had enough time (i.e., not a sudden, unexpected death) and has been given some help in working through the previously described stages, he will reach a stage during which he is neither depressed nor angry about his 'fate,' " Dr. Kübler-Ross observed. She continues by saying, "Acceptance should not be mistaken for a happy stage. It is almost void of feelings. It is as if the pain had gone, the struggle is over, and there comes a time for 'the final rest before the long journey' as one patient phrased it." Kübler-Ross concludes, "There are a few patients who fight to the end, who struggle and keep a hope that makes it almost impossible to reach this stage of acceptance. They are the ones who will say one day, 'I just cannot make it anymore,' the day they stop fighting, the fight is over. In other words, the harder they struggle to avoid inevitable death, the more they try to deny it, the more difficult it will be for them to reach this final stage of acceptance with peace and dignity."

Hope

In her chapter on hope, Dr. Kübler-Ross says, "We have discussed so far the different stages that people go through when they are faced with tragic news—defense mechanisms in psychiatric terms, coping mechanisms to deal with extremely difficult situations. These means will last for different periods of time and will replace each other or exist at times side by side. The one thing that usually persists through all these stages is hope." Further, she states, "It is the hope that occasionally sneaks in, that all this is just like a nightmare and not true." She concludes by saying, "They showed the greatest confidence in the doctors who allowed for such hope—realistic or not—and appreciated it when hope was offered in spite of bad news. . . . If a patient stops expressing hope, it is usually a sign of imminent death."

Included in the concept of hope are Seligman's "controllability" and "predictability." Of controllability he says: "If a person or animal is in a marginal physical stage, weakened by malnutrition or heart disease, a sense of control can mean the difference between living and dying." He reports a study by N. A. Ferrari (1962) on the elderly, and the freedom or lack of freedom they had in choosing whether or not to enter a nursing home. Those who controlled (made their own decisions) when, where, and why they were entering a home, lived the longest time after entering the home. Those who had been forced to enter a home, chosen for them, at a time chosen for them, often died before entry to the home or shortly after. Seligman concludes from this and other studies of both humans and animals that: The amount of control—perceived or real—a person has during a time of crisis or change may make the difference in whether the person goes on to the stage of accepting a new life-style or dying—physically or mentally—in his depression.

Also tied in with hope is predictability. Again, in studies with human and animal subjects, it has been shown that a great deal of trauma and shock can be tolerated and overcome if it is predictable. "In general, men and animals prefer predictable to unpredictable aversive events." In addition, he says, "Studies on humans all find a preference for immediate over delayed shock." He concludes: "So acute fear is preferred to the anxiety or chronic fear that unpredictability produces."

In conclusion, then, a crisis is a disruption of a person's steady state of existence by a changing situation. Just as there is a need to talk about death, it is necessary to discuss divorce, too; divorce is the death of a relationship. Understanding where we are in our crisis—whatever that crisis may be—will help us evaluate our emotional state. Furthermore, it will help us to vent these emotions into nondestructive channels.

Such life changes as death, divorce, pregnancy, and even adoption may have a stressful effect upon us. Negative responses to these stresses can lead to physical illness or emotional illness or possibly suicide. On the other hand, a crisis can be a catalyst that shakes up old habits and forces us to chart new ways. Positive responses can strengthen our potential for a rewarding life and enrich our personality.

We go through various stages in the long process of adjusting to a life-style change; the one thing that usually persists through all these stages is hope. When we have reached the stage of acceptance of the crisis experience, faith develops and growth follows. A new life-style is within our grasp. As Christians we have a certain or "sure" hope. In Hebrews 6:19 we read: "Which hope we have as an anchor of the soul, both sure and stedfast. . . ."

Total the number of life changes you have experienced
within the past year. (Use list of life events and
values.)

Consider the stressful effect of these changes and evaluate your responses as positive or negative.

For at least a year following any major life change,
good or bad, monthly physical checkups may be
warranted.

Find your place on the Crisis Cycle model and date the
period of time when you passed through various
stages. Where are you?

1. *Denial*   Are you still denying that your husband
   divorced you or that your wife died?
2. *Anger*   Can you admit your anger toward God
   for taking your husband so suddenly or anger toward yourself for having a baby when you were
   too young and not married?
3. *Bargaining*   Are you continuing to bargain with
   God? "I promise I will stop nagging if you bring
   him back to me." "I won't go through with the
   divorce proceedings if she says she's sorry."
4. *Depression*   Are you in a state of depression as
   you continue to weigh the fearful price?
5. *Acceptance*   Can you be realistic and begin to
   accept your situation? If you can, you are on your
   way up.

Identify your emotional needs.

Set a goal! Where do you want to be at a certain time?

It isn't what happens to a person that matters so much as how he reacts to what happens to him; and how he reacts will be determined by his inner resources of heart and mind—his fundamental philosophy, his innermost religion, and what he really believes.

We have not been promised easy circumstances, "In this world you will have tribulation." John 16:33.

The personality in which there is conflict is much more likely to give way under the pressure of difficult circumstances than the one which is integrated and truly made whole by the Lord Jesus Christ.

ARTHUR POOL
Consultant Psychiatrist
In the Service of Medicine

7
Emotions Are Signals to Be Heeded

Anger, depression, fear, and other emotions are like red lights signaling us that something is wrong. We need to heed these signals by stopping to see why we are angry, depressed, or fearful, and discover what happens when we allow these emotions to dominate our lives. The emotions we show are not always the emotions we feel internally. For example, after divorce a person may put on an attitude of not caring, when inside he is torn apart.

Anger

Someone has said that bottled anger can kill you. Anger is energy and must be released, but it needs to be directed into appropriate channels.

During summer break, my son Stan worked at a lumberyard. The owner of the business was a cantankerous man who seemed to enjoy making life miserable for everyone. And Stan was an impatient teenager. The combination could have been explosive!

In order to break the tenseness, I picked Stan up for lunch each day. "Take your anger out in appropriate ways," I advised, "but don't take it out on the boss, your family, or friends, and please don't be destructive. Try screaming, or kick the garbage can."

One noon he jumped in the car, rolled down the window, and screamed a hearty teenage scream. Startled, I asked, "What was that all about?" (I had forgotten my own well-intentioned advice). He grinned and replied, "You told me to scream when I got uptight." We both laughed! He survived the summer with not too many battle wounds and had learned an important lesson.

Anger is a reaction to something that damages our prestige. Divorce certainly deflates our egos and prestige. Interestingly enough, death can have the same effect.

At times we use anger when we can't solve our problems. It is, in essence, saying, "I'm defeated."

Sometimes we become angry very quickly; other times our anger develops slowly. The more we suppress anger, the longer it lasts, and the more damage we do to ourselves internally. People who are able to express their anger don't suffer as much physically or emotionally. Anger can punish every member of our body. When it is turned inward we may find ourselves suffering from skin problems, headaches, ulcers, and fatigue.

A person left alone due to a death, divorce, or as an unmarried parent may experience anger. Regrettably, this anger is usually directed toward children, former spouse, lover, or toward oneself. Anger begets anger so that children following in a parent's footsteps may well become angry and hostile also. Because children do model, the single parent needs to be especially aware of anger in himself or in herself. Mothers of small children, particularly, need to guard against harboring anger. A hostile mother is apt to promote hostility in her child. On the other hand, a child smothered by his mother may also be angry and will not learn to be independent. Because they have not resolved their own conflicts, single parents may have a tendency to lean in one direction or the other.

It takes a stable, mature person to stand the freedom of "leisure" without becoming upset. Single parents may find themselves especially irritable and angry on holidays, anniversaries, and weekends, for a variety of reasons (such as not getting away from children for outings or remorse over loss of a mate or lover).

Angry people tend to be negative. This is obvious from their conversation—conversation often centered around their own personal doubts and disappointments. They continue to talk about their former husband or wife, reviewing the good or bad experiences of their married lives. Angry people have a tendency to distrust others; they may also be demanding. Single parents need to heed warning signs so they will not fall into these "anger traps."

Psychologist Alex Shand, in suggesting the types of mothers who produce the most angry children—"cold, demanding ones, syrupy, coddling ones, self-righteous martyred ones"—commented, "Large-minded tolerance, mixed with humor, reasonable perspective of small misdeeds, no nagging afterwards; these result in children who are less frequently angry."

* * *

Ways to Deal With Anger   Whether you are angry over the loss of a mate through death or divorce, an unwanted child, or lack of support from your extended family, realize that anger is normal. Anger in itself is not wrong—it's what we do with anger: ". . . let not the sun go down upon your wrath" (Ephesians 4:26).

Discover why you are angry. Pinpointing your anger will help you to deal with it appropriately. Of course you feel angry because your wife left you for someone else. People may also be angry when a husband or wife dies.

Don't let anger accumulate. Bottled anger either goes inward or else explodes in all directions. Anger should be dealt with as it occurs.

Find appropriate channels for anger. Anger can be converted into success and achievement. There are many legitimate outlets such as golf, piano playing, skiing, scrubbing the kitchen floor, painting or papering a room in the house, weeding the garden, or shoveling the snow.

Fear

A second and equally important emotion is fear. As with anger, fear is also a form of energy. Fear is a response to emergencies. There are two major fears in life: one of death and the other of life.

Dr. Abraham Maslow, psychologist of Brandeis University, wrote of fear:

Each step forward is a step into the unfamiliar and is possibly dangerous. It also means giving up something familiar and good and satisfying. It frequently means a parting and a separation, even a kind of death prior to rebirth, with consequent nostalgia, fear, loneliness and mourning. It also often means giving up a simpler and easier life in exchange for a more demanding, more responsible, and more difficult life.

Some people are naturally more fearful than others. Becoming a single parent is a step into the unfamiliar and brings many fearful moments. Added responsibilities, stress, loneliness, and weariness produce anxiety and fear which eat away at the single parent. Since fear is considered to be contagious, as single parents we need to learn to control and work toward overcoming our own fears so our children will not become fearful.

Eleanor Roosevelt, in her book *You Learn by Living*, has this to say about fear: "You gain strength, courage, and confidence by every experience in which you really stop to look fear in the face. You are able to say, 'I lived through this horror. I can take the next thing that comes along. . . .' You must do the thing you think you cannot do."

Ways to Deal With Fear   How do we do the things we think we cannot do? We need not live in a constant state of fear, but should accept short periods of fear as natural. We respond fearfully to most major changes in our lives such as death, divorce, change of job, pregnancy as a single—or even to a happy event such as marriage or adoption.

Live in the present. *If only I hadn't divorced him. How will I ever be able to earn enough money to put my children through school?* Or, *If only I wasn't pregnant! How can I ever face my friends?* These thoughts are evidence of living in the past or future. There are enough fears today without dwelling on yesterday and tomorrow.

Find a "listener"—someone with whom you can share your fears. Try to locate a person who will help you to be realistic—not one who will criticize your fearful attitude, baby you, or give you false hope. You need a supportive, objective individual during this important stage of your life.

Be sure life is balanced with enough rest, relaxation, good

nourishing food, fun, and fellowship so that you are physically and emotionally fit to face your fear objectively.

Encourage yourself by thinking and talking positively. For example, *I lost my husband, but I have two lovely children, a nice home, and a good job.* Surely you have much to be thankful for.

Force yourself to step out into fearful experiences as Eleanor Roosevelt suggested. Personally, I had to determine to take a trip to New York with my four children, through mountains and on busy expressways, before I realized that I could do it. Act confident, even if you don't feel like it.

The minute you are aware of your fear, begin to deal with it. One of the most important ways to begin to deal with fear is by recognizing the hope we have in God. In Hebrews 6:19 we read that we have this hope as an anchor for the soul, firm and secure. The psalmist in Psalms 56:3 writes: "What time I am afraid, I will trust in thee." The entire chapter of Psalm 46 speaks of the hope we can have in God.

Make a positive effort to relax. When I find myself in a frightening situation I try several things:

* * *

Deep-breathing exercises: Breathe in slowly and exhale several times.

Quote Scripture aloud: Isaiah 26:3, "Thou wilt keep him in perfect peace, whose mind is stayed on thee." Psalms 34:4, "I sought the Lord, and he heard me, and delivered me from all my fears."

Sing or hum songs relating to peace: "Peace, peace, wonderful peace, coming down from the Father above."

Exercise: Outdoor exercise is best—bike riding, walking, swimming, for example. Doing exercises indoors will also be helpful.

Depression

Depression is difficult to deal with and to define because it differs from person to person in depth, duration, and degree. Two definitions of *depression* are:

Depression is an emotional state of dejection and sadness, ranging from mild discouragement and downheartedness to feelings of utter hopelessness and despair.

Depression is exaggerated sadness coupled with pessimism and pessimism is the essential component that distinguishes depression from the ordinary "low" feelings that we all experience from time to time. The depressed person is not simply sad; he has the impression that his sadness will persist indefinitely regardless of what he does about it.

Depression brought on by external situations such as the death of a loved one, divorce, pregnancy, or failure at work are considered *reactive* depressions. But all depressions can be classified as mild, moderate, or severe, regardless of the cause.

All of us experience *mild depressions.* There may be "blue Mondays," low moods, or we feel melancholy and sad from time to time. Sometimes there is a good reason; for example, we may dread a heavy week at work, or a rainy day may make us depressed. Other times, our blues seem to come from nowhere.

Moderate depressions are more intense than mild depressions and may interfere with our homelife or work. Moderate depressions are brought on almost exclusively by a loss or upsetting event. People suffering from this type of depression are often unable to think straight, show great anxiety, and have difficulty conversing without becoming melancholy.

Severe depression brings marked changes in behavior, deep worry, insomnia, and lack of ability to function adequately. "A depression is considered neurotic when the sense of loss is disproportionate to the event that precipitated it, or when the period of dejection goes on indefinitely."

When we are depressed for long periods of time, we need to ask ourselves several questions: *Am I distorting the situation all out of proportion in my mind? What is causing my continued depression? Am I using depression as self-pity or to get pity and sympathy from others?* One traumatic life event is usually not responsible for depression. As cited in chapter six, several stressful events added together over a period of time may bring on severe depression and even illness. It would be most unusual if we did not react to the pressures of single parenting, on occasion, by becoming depressed. Christ Himself was depressed when His disciples could not watch and pray with Him in the garden. He took Peter and James and John and began to be sorrowful and "very heavy." Then He said unto them, "My soul is exceedingly sorrowful, even unto death" (*see* Mark 14:34).

David also expressed his own depressed state in Psalms 77: "My soul refused to be comforted. I complained. My spirit was overwhelmed. I am so troubled that I cannot speak" (*see* verses 2–4).

Depression is a combination of many emotions—anger and hatred toward self, fear of disapproval, loneliness, guilt. A depressed person believes he can't continue alone and may have a poor self-image. Depression is the emotional equivalent of "quitting."

People suffering from depression often have deep feelings of guilt. "I didn't do all I should have for my husband, and he died. I'm a bad person." "If only I had been more tolerant of my wife, she wouldn't have left me. I wonder how she and the children will make it without me?" Depressed people need to understand the difference between real guilt and pseudoguilt; they are usually hostile and turn their hostile feelings toward themselves rather than outwardly venting them.

Another aspect of depression is fear of rejection. Rejection, of course, plays an important role in any divorce. However, people left alone through death often feel rejected also. The unmarried mother may feel rejected by the father of her child, and the single adoptive parent may sense a lack of support from his or her extended family. If a love need has not been met, a person will believe others aren't interested either. Many believe that even God has rejected them and that love is conditional.

Ways to Deal With Depression The depressed person needs someone to react with love and acceptance. He should not simply be told to "snap out of it." He may need firm advice, but it should be given with love and understanding. Feelings of unworthiness, sinfulness, or pseudoguilt can be overcome with supportive counseling. A depressed person needs to recall that God's love is never conditional.

When my father and my mother [husband, wife, children] forsake me, then the Lord will take me up.

Psalms 27:10

Blessed be God, even the Father of our Lord Jesus Christ, the Father of mercies, and the God of all comfort; Who comforteth us in all our tribulation, that we may be able to comfort them which are in any trouble, by the comfort wherewith we ourselves are comforted of God.

2 Corinthians 1:3, 4

Forgiveness

Are you holding a grudge against God for what you consider unfair circumstances in your life? Perhaps you are experiencing remorse, regret, and self-condemnation and are turning your anger inward. Or you may be angry at your mate for divorcing you. Regardless, you must forgive God, others, and yourself before you can begin to heal emotionally, physically, and spiritually.

Corrie ten Boom's touching illustration of forgiveness in *The Hiding Place* is an example of the difficulty involved in forgiveness. How could she possibly forgive the soldiers who made her walk naked before them? One day she found herself talking to one of the soldiers toward whom she felt such bitterness. God gave her grace to forgive, and she experienced peace and healing. She said, "Forgiveness is not an emotion, . . . it is an act of the will."

Dr. Paul Tournier, in *Guilt and Grace* (Harper & Row), says:

The repression of conscience, the reflex of self-justification, and the projection of guilt upon others, are only false solutions to the problem of guilt. They constitute a natural and automatic tendency towards healing, but they solve nothing and they are indeed a hindrance to a true solution since they strengthen self-righteousness. The only true solution, both from the psychological standpoint and in the light of the Bible is the reverse of this, namely, the acceptance of our responsibilities, genuine recognition of our guilt, and repentance and the receiving of God's forgiveness in response to this repentance.

It is abundantly clear that no man lives free of guilt. Guilt is universal. But according as it is repressed or recognized, so it sets in motion one of two contradictory processes: repressed, it leads to anger, rebellion, fear and anxiety, a deadening of conscience, an increasing inability to recognize one's faults, and a growing dominance of aggressive tendencies. But consciously recognized, it leads to repentance, to the peace and security of divine pardon, and in that way to a progressive refinement of conscience and a steady wakening of aggressive impulses.

Maxwell Maltz, in his book *Psycho-Cybernetics,* defines *forgiveness* as a "scalpel which removes emotional scars." Consider forgiveness as Pollyanna Sedziol views it in her poem:

> Forgive us
> ... unless I can forgive this one
> who has hurt me so badly
> rejecting me so fully,
> I can expect nothing less
> than the pain of like rejection
> both now and in eternity, seeing how

God in Christ so fully forgave me
my every rebellion and wrong:
Lord God, I do want to forgive—
remind me, hold me, help me!
as we forgive others.

Emotions may become stepping-stones toward a new
and better life-style. Each step of faith will bring
growth and confidence in yourself and God.

Discover why you are angry. Accept anger as normal
after a crisis.

Deal with anger as it occurs, trying to find appropriate
channels for it.

Accept periods of fear as normal, but deal with fear immediately, too.

Do some serious thinking about why you are fearful.
Are you overly tired? Are there psychological reasons why fear may be greater at this time?

Live in the present. Strive for a balanced life.

Think positively, act confidently. Remember that fearful attitudes may be contagious.

Step out into fearful experiences.

In a frightening situation try techniques that help you
to relax.

Find a nonthreatening listener. If you are depressed,
talk it out with a counselor, minister, or understanding friend.

Admit your depression and realize it is a normal reaction to crisis. Christ was depressed, but He looked
beyond that to "the joy that was set before Him"
(*see* Hebrews 12:2).

Give your depression time to lift naturally. You will
improve as time goes on.
We must forgive before we can be healed. "Forgiveness is a scalpel which removes emotional scars."
Trust in the God of all comfort. Realize that His Love
is unconditional.

Suggested Reading

Augsburger, David. *Caring Enough to Confront.* Rev. ed. Scotts-
dale, Pa.: Herald Press, 1980.

Carlson, Dwight L. *How to Win Over Fatigue.* Old Tappan, N.J.:
Fleming H. Revell, 1980.

Lewis, C. S. *The Problem of Pain.* New York: Macmillan, 1943.

Narramore, Bruce, and Counts, Bill. *Freedom From Guilt.* Santa
Ana, Calif.: Vision House, 1974.

Tournier, Paul. *Guilt and Grace.* New York: Harper & Row,
1962.

The language of the body has a quality of unmatched validity.... The body is as much a part of the individual as the mind, the emotions; the personality expresses itself through all its elements.

ALLAN FROMME
The Ability to Love

8
Sexuality and the Single Parent

To say there is no sexual adjustment after an individual becomes single is to hide one's head in the sand, like the proverbial ostrich, and say it doesn't exist. When separation deprives an individual of this important aspect of a marriage relationship, common sense tells us there must be a void. It matters not whether it is a man or a woman, whether the marriage has been for one or fifty years, or whether the separation has come about through death, divorce, or desertion. There is a void!

The naivete of some Christians regarding sexuality, even in this so-called enlightened age, is appalling. For example, one well-educated woman approached me after reading the above statement and commented, "You know, I never realized sex was a problem for single parents."

On another occasion a Christian psychologist speaking at a single's conference was questioned by a widower, "How does one handle his sexual drives as a single?" "Well," replied the psychologist, "you handle them the same way I do. I travel a great deal and am away from home for days, sometimes weeks, at a time. You abstain." Obviously his answer left much to be desired. Conference attendees realized his situation wasn't quite the same as theirs; he would eventually go home to his wife.

Far from being naive, however, are some Christians who become so "knowledgeable" and taken up with the world's point of view that they have conveniently forgotten or rationalized away what the Bible says about sex. Recently a Christian college graduate, since divorced and remarried, startled me by saying, "In counseling young people, I encourage them to have premarital sex. It's better to find out if you're compatible before marriage. Besides, it makes adjustment to marriage easier." This man, along with many other Christians, is allowing the world to "mold" his sexual orientation and behavior.

This type of advice, coming from a Christian, seems so less than Christian; but what can you expect when everyone, singles and single parents alike, have become prime targets for naturalistic sexual exploitation. They are being bombarded with *SEX,* sometimes with disgusting frankness. Imagine a huge billboard, placed so the public must see it blocks away, picturing a scantily clad female or a handsome, muscular male, smiling and saying, in essence, "Look like me and do the things I do, and you'll be successful, too!" Other times exploitation is so subtle that viewers are not conscious of what's happening. Advertisers know, however, that the sexual image they plant is being subconsciously stored in the viewer's mind, right where they want it!

Industry has recently discovered the potential spending power of the growing population of singles, single parents, and their children. This discovery has sparked a massive advertising program designed to reach this very special group. Now we're advised that everything from wearing snug-fitting jeans to drinking wine is the "thing to do." ("It's downright upright for a single woman to ask a man over for a drink.")

Television is also gearing more and more programs to singles and single parents. One such program entitled *Sex, and the Single Parent* was, fortunately, short-lived. Books and magazines continue to discuss intimate subjects such as "The Ingenious Sex Lives of Divorced Mothers" (*Cosmopolitan,* January, 1976). The author of this particular article described the unhappy sexual state of the divorced woman by saying, "Juggling a single woman's sex life with the demands of children can sometimes make you feel so incredibly hassled that all you want to do is burrow into bed and dream about running off to Guadalupe with Robert De-Niro."

Teenagers' problems are being compounded not only because of this constant emphasis on sex, but also because many adults provide no clear standards regarding morality and sexual behavior. An article in *Families* magazine (May, 1981) "Teen-agers and Sex: The Price of Freedom" describes this confusion, "Some parents and educators see this reckless Sybaritism of the young as a fallout from a decade of social upheavals; women's liberation; the exploding divorce rate; the decline of parental and institutional authority; the widespread acceptance of 'living together.' The sexual revolution, they note, has also provided an unwitting new model for teens. 'There are a lot of divorced and single parents dating,' says Judith Gorbach, Director of Family Planning for the Massachusetts Department of Public Health. 'The message everywhere is sex.' "

Is it any wonder then that: (1) the number of sexually active teenagers increased by two-thirds in the seventies and that 12 million teenagers out of a total of 29 million between the ages of thirteen and nineteen had sexual intercourse or (2) that one poll, interviewing women ages eighteen and up, found that 61 percent of single and 51 percent of divorced women polled maintain that premarital sex is not necessarily immoral?

The so-called sexual freedom our society has been indulging in has not brought freedom, but has rather left its victims empty, guilty, lonely, and in bondage. Dwight Hervey Small, in his book *Christian: Celebrate Your Sexuality,* paints a vivid picture of this bondage, "Sex by itself, apart from marital bonds, stands starkly as the symbol of personal impoverishment."

Fortunately, the Christian single parent: widowed, divorced, separated, unmarried, or single adoptive, has a positive alternative to this impoverishment. Dr. M. O. Vincent, in his book *God, Sex and You,* suggests that "The Christian's moral life is the outgrowth of a new relationship to God through Jesus Christ. This personal relationship is the sure foundation of all Christian conduct." He goes on to explain to the individual who is not a Christian that "since this is the cornerstone, it is impossible to live a life ethically pleasing to God without this prior relationship. Our moral life is because we are Christian, not that our conduct makes us Christian." Now this does not suggest that Christians do not sin, but rather that the Christian has Someone to turn to for help. Jesus Christ is understanding, unconditionally loving and forgiving, and will provide positive direction for anyone who desires it. The Christian single parent also has the Bible, which offers extensive information and guidelines to help single parents understand God's will so they may live according to His higher standards.

Since the Bible is so important to the believer, let's consider what it has to say:

I God Created Us as Sexual Beings

Human sexuality was designed by God and is a God-endowed factor of personality. God created mankind in two sexes, as indicated in Mark 10:6: "But from the beginning of the creation God made them male and female." We are therefore sexual beings with different biological drives. God, not man, created sex. It is one of God's good gifts to mankind.

II God Created Us in His Image

"So God created man in his own image, in the image of God created he him...," Genesis 1:27 tells us. Being created in the image of God, though I cannot begin to treat the theological implications, does at least speak of the supreme value of the individual to God. Human beings are not creatures whose role is merely to fulfill biological needs. God transcends biology and physiology. Now since God places such high value on us, His special creations, does it not follow that He would naturally want the best for us: spiritually, emotionally, socially, and even sexually? that He would provide guidelines for us to live our lives as He intended?

Perhaps part of our problem in making moral judgments and decisions is that we have not recognized our intrinsic value to God, nor have we understood the true meaning of being "made in the image of God." I recall counseling a young man in his early twenties. He was very withdrawn, but appeared eager to learn and become more outgoing. After one session in which we discussed the individual's importance to God, I requested that he study the principles regarding self-esteem, from the Bible, for the next few days. When he returned, I asked, "What was helpful to you in your study this week?" His eyes sparkled as he replied, "I never knew I was valuable to anyone before."

Plato spoke of the body as a *tomb*. Paul, the New Testament apostle, in his first letter to the Corinthians (3:16) called the body a *temple*. "Know ye not that ye are the temple of God, and that the Spirit of God dwelleth in you?" How one views one's body, tomb or temple, should make a difference in how one lives.

III God Instituted Marriage at Creation

God spoke of Adam and Eve, in Genesis 2:25, as "the man and his wife." This relationship was designed for a number of very special reasons:

A. *Companionship*. Companionship was one of God's prime motives in bringing Adam and Eve together, as we discover in Genesis 2:18: "And the Lord God said, It is not good that the man should be alone; I will make him an help meet [helper, counterpart] for him." If this important aspect of a marriage relationship were to be more strongly developed, perhaps there would be fewer divorces and separations.

B. *Sexual intimacy*. Sexual intercourse should be the fullest expression of mutual love between husband and wife, according to Proverbs 5:18, 19; 1 Corinthians 7:3–5; Hebrews 13:4, and as expressed in the beautiful love story recorded in the Song of Solomon. Genesis 2:24 defines this physical union as "they shall be one flesh" and "a man ... shall cleave unto his wife." *Cleave* literally means "glued together." It also suggests a lasting or permanent relationship.

C. *Procreation.* In Genesis 1:28 God commanded his new creations to "Be fruitful, and multiply, and replenish the earth. . . ." In Genesis 4:1, 2 we learn that Adam and Eve did as they were instructed, "And Adam knew Eve his wife; and she conceived, and bare Cain. . . . And she again bare his brother Abel. . . ."

So you see marriage in the beginning was characterized by loving companionship, physical intimacy, and procreation.

IV God Intended That Sexual Intimacies Occur Only Within the Marriage Bond

A. The seventh commandment warns, "Thou shalt not commit adultery" (Exodus 20:14).

B. Paul also gave warnings about promiscuity: ". . . Now the body is not for fornication, but for the Lord; and the Lord for the body." "Flee fornication," we are advised. For, "Every sin that a man doeth is without the body; but he that committeth fornication sinneth against his own body" (1 Corinthians 6:13, 18).

C. Promiscuity, in the Bible, is incompatible with personal holiness and is contrary to God's will: ". . . Ye ought to walk and to please God, so ye would abound more and more. . . . ye should abstain from fornication" (1 Thessalonians 4:1, 3). "But fornication and all uncleanness,... let it not be once named among you, as becometh saints" (Ephesians 5:3). "Set your affection on things above, not on things on the earth," and "Mortify therefore your members which are upon the earth; fornication, uncleanness, inordinate affection, evil concupiscence . . ." (Colossians 3:2, 5). (*See also* Galatians 5:16, 19–21; Genesis 12:10–20; Genesis 20:1–18; Genesis 26:6–11.)

V Sexual Sins Are Not "Unpardonable"

A. Sexual sins are listed along with sins such as foolish talking, jesting, anger, wrath, malice, blasphemy, filthy communication, and lying in Colossians 3:5–9 and Ephesians 5:3, 4.

B. Jesus forgave the woman taken in adultery, in John 8:1–11. When she acknowledged Him as Lord, He declared, ". . . Neither do I condemn thee; go, and sin no more."

C. Jesus also forgave the prostitute in Luke 7:36–50. Religious leaders were unhappy with Jesus because He allowed this woman to wash His feet with tears and then wipe them with her hair. She also kissed and anointed His feet with ointment. One of the religious leaders grumbled; "This man, if he were a prophet, would have known who and what manner of woman this is that toucheth him; for she is a sinner." Jesus confronted the unloving crowd by saying, ". . . Her sins, which are many, are forgiven; for she loved much. . . ." Turning to the prostitute, He

said, "Thy sins are forgiven.... thy faith hath
saved thee; go in peace." Jesus made it very clear
that it was her faith, not her works, that saved her.

D. David's story in 2 Samuel 11, 12 is the classic example of man's sin and God's forgiveness. David's
problems began when he ". . . arose from off his
bed, and walked upon the roof of the king's house:
and from the roof he saw a woman washing herself;
and the woman was very beautiful to look upon"
(11:2). If David had only looked, he probably
would have been spared a great deal of heartache.
Unfortunately, "David sent and enquired after the
woman" (verse 3); "David sent messengers, and
took her" (verse 4); and "the woman conceived"
(verse 5). But the tragedy didn't end there. David
then tried to cover his sin by sending Bathsheba's
husband to the front line of battle, and Uriah was
killed. David suffered the consequences of his sins
(as we all do). His child died. Ultimately David
confessed his sin and repented, and God forgave
him: "I acknowledged my sin unto thee, and mine
iniquity have I not hid. I said, I will confess my
transgressions unto the Lord; and thou forgavest
the iniquity of my sin" (Psalms 32:5, *see also* Psalm
51).

So you see, the Bible tells us that there is forgiveness with
God! Just as those in the Scriptures, though correctly re-
ferred to as sinners, found forgiveness with God, so may
the single parent who has erred. The following steps will be
helpful in the process of restoration:

A. *Confess your sins to God.* "If we confess our sins, he is faithful and just to forgive us our sins, and to cleanse us from all unrighteousness" (1 John 1:9).

B. *Commit your life (sex included) to God.* "Keep yourselves in the love of God ..." (Jude 21). "Flee also youthful lusts ..." (2 Timothy 2:22). "Likewise, reckon ye also yourselves to be dead indeed unto sin, but alive unto God, through Jesus Christ our Lord" (Romans 6:11).

C. *Control your thoughts.* John Stott, in *Your Mind Matters* (Inter-Varsity Press), contends that the "battle is nearly always won in the mind." The Bible has a great deal to say about the mind. For example: "I beseech you therefore, brethren, by the mercies of God, that ye present your bodies a living sacrifice, holy, acceptable unto God, which is your reasonable service. And be not conformed to this world: but be ye transformed by the renewing of your mind, that ye may prove what is that good, and acceptable, and perfect, will of God" (Romans 12:1, 2); "... bringing into captivity every thought to the obedience of Christ" (2 Corinthians 10:5); "Wherefore gird up the loins of your mind ... As obedient children, not fashioning yourselves according to the former lusts in your ignorance" (1 Peter 1:13, 14).

D. *Count on God to help you.* Obviously God wants you, His special creation, to be successful. Paul assures you in Philippians 2:13 (TLB) that "... God is at work within you, helping you want to obey him, and then helping you do what he wants." You are further counseled that "There hath no temptation taken you but such as is common to man; but *God is faithful,* who will not suffer you to be tempted above that ye are able; but will with the temptation also make a way to escape, that ye may be able to bear it" (1 Corinthians 10:13, *italics added*).

E. *Contact with an empathetic church and understanding Christians will provide spiritual food and fellowship necessary for continued growth.* Fortunately, more and more Christians and organizations are becoming aware of the growing numbers of single parents and their children. They are also beginning to recognize both their potential and their need. Still, many are lagging behind and not fulfilling their obligations to the single parent. It's for sure, Christian society must consider its responsibility to help those individuals who have erred. Paul does not hesitate to instruct us, "Brethren, if a man be overtaken in a fault, ye which are spiritual, restore such an one in the spirit of meekness; considering thyself, lest thou also be tempted" (Galatians 6:1). Gordon Scorer offers good advice in his book *The Bible and Sex Ethics Today* (Inter-Varsity Press): "Human beings always have done wrong. We are all tarred with the same brush and it is hypocritical to pretend we are better than we are.... What matters is not so much what we are as what we may by God's grace become."

To be sure, Christ came not only to insure eternal life after death for the single parent who is a child of God, but also to provide that person with strength, wisdom, and power to live an abundant life here on earth. Three verses from the Bible that have been especially helpful to me when I needed an extra spiritual boost are found in Ephesians 3:20, 21 and Philippians 4:13. They read, "Now unto him that is able to do exceeding abundantly above all that we ask or think, according to the *power* that worketh in us," and, "I can do all things through Christ which strengtheneth me."

Love is life's greatest experience. To the Christian single parent, love must be viewed, as we've learned, from a different perspective from the world's. Though we cannot totally understand God's love, it should motivate us to greater creativity throughout life—single or married, and with or without sexual intimacy.

A maturing love toward God will help us direct our thoughts to others and motivate us to action in their regard. As you channel sexual energy in a positive direction you will not only experience a deeper commitment and love toward God and others, but you will also discover you are able to use your abilities in creative ways not realized before. For example, homes and hospitals are full of sick people who also need help and encouragement. Doing the laundry; cleaning a house; going shopping or preparing a lovely meal for another person going through a crisis experience; teaching the handicapped a creative craft; reading to the aged or blind; opening your home to young people; using your car to transport people to doctors, hospitals, or meetings; sending letters and cards, or telephoning those in need are a few options for the creative use of one's energy. Or you might want to use this time in your life to develop an area you've always wanted to pursue: a hobby, music, college, teaching, sewing, carpentry, arts, crafts, or travel.

Potentially, you may discover that life is more satisfying and rewarding than you ever dreamed it could be!

Recognize that you are a sexual being and have a natural instinct for physical love.

Desiring physical love is normal. The right and wrong of the matter lies with the way you cope with the desire.

Deepening relationships with a few special people will provide some satisfaction.

Channel sexual energy in a positive direction.

Accept God's forgiveness and forgive yourself, if you have sinned and repented.

Use biblical thought control.

Be confident that God will not leave you and will provide ways to help you.

Suggested Reading

Ketterman, Grace H. *How to Teach Your Child About Sex.* Old Tappan, N.J.: Fleming H. Revell, 1981.

Narramore, Clyde M. *How to Tell Your Children About Sex.* Grand Rapids: Zondervan, 1965.

Small, Dwight Hervey. *Christian: Celebrate Your Sexuality.* Old Tappan, N.J.: Fleming H. Revell, 1974.

Vincent, M. O. *God, Sex and You.* Nashville: A. J. Holman, 1976.

Times of general calamity and confusion have ever been productive of the greatest minds. The purest ore is from the hottest furnace, and the brightest thunderbolt from the darkest cloud.

CHARLES CALEB COLTON

9
Transition Period

The transition from being married to being single is traumatic. The abruptness with which some are thrown into a state of singleness may make life even more catastrophic.

Our minds and bodies do not automatically push a button which says, MARRIED or SINGLE. After being married for one year, or for twenty years, we continue to think *married*. It is also very difficult to think *single* with children dashing about the house.

Just as it took time to adjust to being married after being single for so many years, it will be difficult to adjust to being single again after being married. But the single state in which you find yourself is not at all like the single state you experienced before marriage.

Those individuals who are unmarried parents or single adoptive parents are also in transition. Their transition, however, takes them from a single state to one in which they suddenly find themselves with a family.

Regardless of category, you will find your life-style changing. You are now in a special category, one not really well-defined by society.

For Widowed and Divorced Women Only

Society is usually elated when a baby arrives on the scene, and the new mother is showered with attention. However, a woman entering a new life as a widow or divorcée finds little or no assistance from either individuals or institutions, and her needs are probably greater than that of the new mother.

Becoming a widow or divorcée involves more than losing a husband. A woman may also suffer other losses, such as a drop in income, loss of familiar friends, and possibly loss of the family home. If her husband had been a helpful partner she may have lost a gardener, repairman, or auto mechanic, depending on which roles he performed.

Women probably experience more role changes in life than men do, and these sometimes-disconnected changes may result in a lowered self-esteem. The role changes the single parent is required to make will add greater strain—a further blow to an ego that is already somewhat shattered.

Identity, which is the development of a sense of self, is important throughout life. Who am I? Where am I going in life? What should I be as a woman? a single parent? These questions are important as we seek to establish a new way of life.

Developing a clear sense of identity takes time and should have a good beginning in childhood; ideally it should have been established in the home. Unfortunately, many homes do not provide a setting in which a youngster may develop a strong self-image.

Besides having a good self-concept, a woman should also have several outlets, or props, in life. If one prop is snatched away—her husband—other props will be readily available to her because they have become an established part of her life. This is not to say that she will not miss her husband, but it does mean that she will be better able to cope with what life brings her.

Adaptability, versatility, and a good self-concept, plus

several outlets—these form a solid foundation on which to build a new life. A woman will not feel quite so "stripped" if she has such a foundation on which to rely.

If a woman has not developed a strong sense of identity as a child or before marriage, she may have real difficulty in feeling like a "whole person" after she has been left alone. Because of this "half-person" feeling, she may rely on others—unnecessarily—to bring meaning to her life.

This reliance may be expressed in trying to lose herself in her family. Becoming completely absorbed in one's family is neither satisfying nor healthy for the mother or her children. Children are separate, independent individuals and should constantly be encouraged to work themselves out of and away from the nest. To cling to a child is to dwarf both parent and child.

It is exciting and satisfying to know that children are ready to leave home as independent, capable adults and that we have had a part in helping them become mature persons.

As children become older we cannot expect them to be in the home as much as they were when they were younger, nor will a parent be going as many places with them as one did earlier in life. Schedules cannot always be coordinated for the togetherness shared earlier. More important, however, is the scriptural truth that it is normal and necessary for children to grow up and "leave father and mother" and enter into their own independent lives.

A single mother may want to think of new ways to fill her time as she adjusts to her children leaving home. Entertaining friends once again, for example, may be a satisfying experience. Sometimes we forget what fun it is to have a barbecue, buffet, or fancy dinner party. Sprucing up ourselves and our home may be just the thing to get us out of the self-pity syndrome—"poor me, my children are all leaving home"—and into a new and exciting life.

A single woman may also rely on widows or single women's groups. To do so may only reinforce a poor self-concept and negative feelings toward the rest of the world: "No one cares about me anyway." A woman will certainly want to have widows, divorcées, and other single women as friends, but not to the isolation of other groups of people. Isolation and selectivity may generate greater loneliness and hostility and further delay a healthy adjustment to a new life.

There is also the woman who may find it very difficult to make friends with other single women. One reason is that much of her life has been centered around her husband and children. A second reason may be that she resents being labeled widow or divorcée.

To isolate oneself *from* such groups or to isolate oneself *to* such groups may mean the loss of meaningful relationships. It is better to begin to develop new attitudes about people— not thinking of them in terms of *men, women,* or *children,* but as *persons.*

Eventually a single woman may want to develop relationships with men. A single woman must realize that society allows single men more freedom to meet new people than it does single women. Then, too, there are more women available to the single male. To further narrow the field for a single woman, we find that an older man may date a younger woman without fear of reprisal, but society, in general, still frowns upon an older woman dating a younger man.

The world is becoming somewhat more tolerant toward women who actively seek legitimate relationships with men, but most women are still very hesitant to be assertive in this area. The story of Naomi poses an interesting example of a godly woman who actively sought out a legitimate relationship with a godly man for her daughter-in-law, Ruth. Can't you just hear the little community buzzing with the news, "Did you hear about Ruth and Naomi?" "Can you imagine two widows being so forward?" "Frankly, I think it is just plain disgusting." I wonder if God smiled just a wee bit at the attitudes and inhibitions displayed by the onlookers? Since Naomi's plan was God-ordained, I assume we may accept her behavior as correct.

An older single woman may feel rather foolish as a relationship develops with a man. She may even express herself as "feeling like a teenager again." There may be some hesitancy about entering into a dating relationship because she does not want a man to think of her—at least to begin with—as a potential marriage partner. Usually a woman who has been married has a well-defined idea of what she wants in a future mate. She certainly does not want to intentionally hurt a man's feelings by turning him down, nor does she want him to think she is interested in him if she is not. Mature people do not take dating lightly.

Demands on a single woman may require new attitudes toward tasks her husband formerly performed and that she may consider unfeminine. These tasks may include writing checks, balancing the budget, taking the car to the garage for a tune-up, handling household repairs, and dozens of other roles not previously performed by her.

Personally, I believe that children should learn to do many tasks as they grow up in the comfortable setting of their home. These tasks should not be labeled MALE, FEMALE or MOTHER, FATHER. Girls should be allowed to watch and help father fix a lamp, hang a picture, change a tire, or balance a budget. Boys should know how to sort, wash, and dry the laundry, press a shirt, bake a cake, and shop for groceries.

Children who are brought up knowing how to do many tasks and to perform a variety of roles will not find it so difficult to adjust to marriage, nor will separation from a mate, should that occur, be such a shattering experience.

If a woman already feels comfortable driving a car, paying bills, or confronting the garage mechanic, she will not be quite so frustrated if she should need to seek employment after becoming single again. Every woman should continue to develop her skills and talents throughout marriage. She will then have these resources to draw upon if she is faced with raising her family alone.

How thankful I was for my typing and shorthand skills. A short brush-up course was all I needed to get me started in a new profession. As an extra bonus I was able to give piano lessons. This not only helped us financially but it also gave me added assurance that I was a capable person and, furthermore, that I could trust God to help me in my new role as a single parent.

For Widowed and Divorced Men Only

Men, too, must adjust to a new life-style after becoming single parents. The transition may be different from that of a woman, but it is very real, and just as difficult.

Men usually have more continuity in their life-style from youth to old age than women do. Their identity, including roles such as husband, father, wage earner, and sportsman, has been established, so they may not feel quite so fragmented after being left alone.

A woman, on the other hand, as has already been suggested, often feels like a "half-person" after a divorce or the death of her husband.

Feeling comfortable in an already settled occupation relieves a man of much of the stress and strain usually required of a woman when she becomes single. But the life of the single male parent is not "all joy." He has some particular problems and adjustments that a woman does not have.

Men may have to learn to perform so-called feminine roles. A man may never have had to prepare a meal, do the laundry, grocery shop, or vacuum the carpet. On top of feeling rejected and less masculine, he may also feel very foolish and angry because he is obligated to assume these unfamiliar tasks.

Though men experience loneliness and grief just as much as women do, society has not allowed them to express grief and loneliness by crying. Men, as you know, are supposed to be strong, unemotional, silent, and aggressive. This unnecessary standard puts undue stress and strain on a single man as he seeks to adjust. He may try to run away from his true feelings, or escape into the past, since he is not supposed to express his feelings in legitimate ways.

Edward Dayton in an essay "On Learning to Cry" says:

> I don't know when I learned to cry. . . . Perhaps it just happens as you grow older. Life is never easy for a young man, I suspect. No matter how outwardly confident he appears, inside is the fear—the fear of the unknown that lies ahead, the fear of not being accepted, of being "different," or

being rejected. But tears, after all, are for children.... I wish I had learned to cry sooner. And I wish our society would let me cry more.

A male single parent may have to make some major financial adjustments. Left alone through the death of his wife, a widower may have to hire a housekeeper, adding financial strain.

A divorced man, on the other hand, has alimony and child support to pay. Child-support payments are not tax deductible; his salary is now taxed at a higher rate; and he is maintaining two households instead of one. But, he is still on the same salary.

The single male parent has other problems also. He may work many hours a day, possibly to help with the added expenses, or perhaps as an escape. Regardless of the reason, work may become all-consuming but far from satisfying.

For a time, after the loss of his wife, a divorced man may find the company of "the boys" enjoyable; he may even boast about how great his freedom is, but he soon finds this kind of life boring and drab.

The single male, entering into a new social life again, finds it as unfamiliar to him as it is to the single woman. He may, in fact, be very fearful of any kind of a relationship with a woman. For example, a very sincere, innocent, compliment may be taken more seriously by a woman than was intended, so the man backs off from what should have been a natural expression of appreciation.

A man, fearing rejection, may also be afraid to ask a woman for a date. Rejection would add to his already diminished masculinity and ego. He may especially fear seeking the companionship of an attractive, assertive type of woman, even though he may honestly want to get to know her better.

A divorced man struggles with guilt feelings along with a real sense of loss—especially in regard to his children. Though he wants a loving, meaningful relationship with them, he finds it extremely difficult when he sees them only on weekends or once a month. He must realize that it is the quality of the time spent with his children, not the quantity, that is important.

Sexual adjustment will probably be more difficult for the single male than the female. In fact, he may find it difficult to maintain a proper relationship with a woman companion. "... the general public is rarely shocked by, or may even expect and be tolerant of, some measure of sexual activity in single middle-aged males, regardless of the nature of the relationship," states P. H. Gebhardt in a lecture delivered at the Institute for Sex Research on the campus of the University of Indiana in 1974.

Though research data indicates that women tolerate periods of little or no sexual activity better than men do, the following information was also cited by Mr. Gebhardt in the same address, "There are indications that nearly all divorced females resume sexual activity following the divorce, as compared with about 50 percent of widows. Widows usually are more financially secure, and are subtly inhibited through continuing bonds with in-laws from engaging in sex with other men."

The Christian must recognize the scriptural teaching that "continence is appropriate" regardless of society's view on the subject. But further, as Dr. Roger Crook stated in *An Open Book to the Christian Divorcée*, "... sex without commitment is fundamentally unsatisfactory. . . . To be fundamentally satisfying, sexual intercourse demands love, acceptance, and commitment."

Single Adoptive Parents Only

Regardless of the joy a child may bring into the life of the single person who has dreamed of parenting, major adjustments must be expected for both parent and child. Since older and physically/emotionally handicapped children are usually placed with single adoptive parents, the time required for proper adjustment may be longer. Older children, for example, generally present more adjustment difficulties, simply because the child's personality has already developed to a great extent. Many older children have also had earlier experiences of deprivation, abuse, and instability and come to the single parent with substantially more emotional problems. The physically handicapped child may require an even greater amount of care—perhaps lifelong.

Adjustment of both parent and child are dependent on several factors. Much of the responsiblity for good adjustment depends on the parent's own sense of well-being and self-esteem. Research indicates that single adoptive parents take longer to consider a child their own than couples who adopt and that males take longer to adjust to parenting than females.

The fact that you, the single adoptive parent, will have a significantly restricted social life after a child arrives must be accepted as part of this newly chosen life-style. Understandably, there aren't too many other single adoptive parents with whom to socialize; you may not quite fit into the divorced or widowed single-parent group; married couples may not be ready to accept you; and your single friends don't feel comfortable talking about, or being around, children. Now, instead of accepting social invitations, you may find yourself saying more often: "I've got to attend a parent-teacher conference tonight." "Sorry, I can't make it. Johnny's sick." "I'm short on cash this week." "The house needs cleaning." Or, "Sally needs help with her math." Your social life may include much more family time, both your own and extended-family involvements.

Extended-family relationships are extremely important. When extended families respond positively, there is better adjustment, sooner, for both parent and child.

The major new tasks faced by the single adoptive parent, their costs, and time commitments may loom especially large in this transitional stage.

For Unmarried Parents Only

Though the number of unmarried parents is escalating and it seems commonplace for children to be born of these relationships, the transition from the life of a relatively "free" teenager to the life of a teenager with a child is overwhelming.

The freedom a teenager may have hoped to find by having a baby just doesn't exist. If she felt confined before, she will feel controlled now. If she stays at home, her mother usually becomes the child's parent. If, on the other hand, she moves away and lives alone, she is trapped by the baby and other responsibilities. Should she decide to finish school, she may find added responsibilities at home make it impossible to study. Dating could be a major problem. Some fellows may ask for a date only for what they can get. Others don't want to date a girl with a baby. Now she can't just say, "I'm going out for the evening," but rather, "Where will I get money for a baby-sitter?" and, "Who will take care of the baby for me?" Babies aren't too popular when taken on dates.

The transitions:

from going to the department store for a new dress	to not being able to afford one because baby needs food and clothing
from always being with so-called special friends	to being ignored or rejected
from saying, "Hey, Dad, how about ten dollars"	to working for that same ten dollars
from spending hours on oneself	to changing and washing diapers, rocking baby, getting up in the middle of the night

are all issues that must now be dealt with on a moment-by-moment basis.

The young unmarried parent has had little experience at fulfilling day-in-and-day-out adult responsibilities. Because of this, the presence of support and mature parenting examples from church, community, and family can make the difference between failure as a parent and transition from teenager to successful parent.

Time management and finances are critical concerns of all single parents. Helpful information on these two subjects is provided in chapter twelve, "Society and the Single Parent."

Recognize that you are in transition—"going from one life-style to another."

Look upon your transition period as a challenge. The new life-style may very well be a great improvement over the old.

God can help and will help as you seek His will through prayer, Bible study, Christian counsel, and Christian friends.

Remember that God also expects you to help yourself.

Suggested Reading

Atkin, Edith and Rubin, Estelle. *Part-Time Father*. New York: Vanguard Press, 1976.

Bel Geddes, Joan. *How to Parent Alone: A Guide for Single Parents*. New York: Seabury Press, 1974.

Duty, Guy. *Divorce and Remarriage*. Minneapolis: Bethany Fellowship, 1967.

Edwards, Marie, and Hoover, Eleanor. *The Challenge of Being Single*. New York: New American Library, 1975.

Halverson, Richard C. *Perspective: Devotional Thoughts for Men*. Grand Rapids: Zondervan, 1970.

———. *Be Yourself and God's*. Grand Rapids: Zondervan, 1971.

Hensley, J. Clark. *Help for Single Parents*. Jackson, Miss.: Christian Action Commission, 1973.

Hosier, Helen Kooiman. *The Other Side of Divorce*. Nashville: Abingdon, 1975.

Johnson, Barbara Mary. *Saying Yes to Change*. Minneapolis: Augsburg, 1982.

Landorf, Joyce. *The Fragrance of Beauty*. Wheaton, Ill.: Victor Books, 1973.

————. *The Richest Lady in Town.* Grand Rapids: Zondervan, 1979.

McGinnis, Marilyn A. *Single.* New York: Jove, 1976.

Peppler, Alice Stolper. *Single Again—This Time with Children.* Minneapolis: Augsburg, 1982.

Petersen, Evelyn R., and Petersen, J. Allan. *The Fine Art of Being a Woman.* Wheaton, Ill.: Tyndale House, 1974.

Petersen, J. Allan. *The Dynamics of Being a Man and Succeeding at It.* Wheaton, Ill.: Tyndale House, 1973.

Robison, James. *In Search of a Father.* Wheaton, Ill., Tyndale House, 1980.

Small, Dwight H. *The Right to Remarry.* Old Tappan, N.J.: Fleming H. Revell, 1975.

The sorrow which has no vent in tears may make other organs weep.

HENRY MAUDSLEY

10
Parental Behavior Problems

"I can't believe I'm behaving as I am," Chris sobbed. "I act worse than my children. Will I ever get it all together again?"

I assured Chris that somewhere along the way life would take on new meaning as she successfully worked through the frustration of raising her children alone.

Single parents are not the only ones who experience behavior problems. Their problems, however, often appear worse and surface more frequently simply because the single parent has much added responsibility which he or she must now bear alone.

For example, single mothers are often blamed for problems with boys in particular. One mother, raising a son alone, may feel very inadequate for the task ahead of her. Another mother, on the other hand, may not want help in raising her son. She may feel quite capable and resent any intrusion into her life. Both mothers need guidance. Their attitudes indicate lack of understanding of their own needs as well as of the needs of their sons. Boys need mature, responsible, and active adult male models. Mothers cannot fill this need. A mother may overprotect her son, or she may make him the man of the house. Both approaches are unhealthy for a growing boy.

If a mother has hostile feelings toward men, she may express her hostility by putting down her son or nagging him. The mother's hostile feelings may cause her son to have feelings of inferiority and worthlessness. A boy needs to know his maleness is good, a thing to be developed and encouraged.

A single parent may treat a child of the opposite sex as a date. Or a father may expect a daughter to fill the role his wife formerly held and find himself putting too much pressure on her regarding household responsibilities. Neither behavior is acceptable. Adolescence is difficult at best without adding these pressures.

A widow, unable to attend college herself, attempted to live through her daughter. The daughter became frustrated because she could not live up to her mother's ideal, gave up in despair, and left college.

A divorcée attempted to substitute prayer and Bible reading for active faith, avoiding interaction with others. As she became more withdrawn from society, she fantasized that a famous movie actor was going to marry her. She could not cope with the trauma and rejection of divorce. Her son also suffered emotional problems, and became a drug abuser.

Mary, a middle-aged widow, left her husband's study exactly as it was when Bill died. His coat was tossed carelessly across a chair; and books, papers, and letters were strewn on top of his desk. Mary lived in a world of make-believe, hoping Bill would return and life would go on without interruption. This was, of course, not a normal home situation for children to grow up in.

Some special problems single parents may experience are manipulation, martyrdom, and psychosomatic ailments.

Manipulation

To *manipulate,* according to the dictionary, is "to manage by clever use of personal influence, especially unfair influence." There is danger in manipulating or using another person as a prop for one's own ego. Emotional murder is committed when we treat another individual as an *it* or a *thing* because we are denying him his God-given right to his unique personhood.

A single parent may find himself manipulating his child to get him to perform a certain task. Or a parent may find himself giving in to his child's desires (even though these desires are not acceptable), to get him to respond. Then there is the mother who cries and says, "How could you do that to me?" The child, feeling guilty because he made his mother sad, gives in to his mother's tears. Crying is okay, but crying to manipulate is not.

One mother became skilled at manipulating her sons after their father's death. She had good training, for her parents and husband had allowed her to manipulate them. Her sons became easy prey and were manipulated without too much effort. This was the pattern of behavior they grew up with. Her most effective trick was to feign a sick spell; the boys would rush to her aid, reinforcing her ability to manipulate people. These spells often came at a time when her sons were about to make a decision that was not to her liking or when someone else held the center of the stage in her sons' thinking. Both sons suffered deep emotional conflicts. True to form they, too, manipulate other people.

Martyrdom

A person assumes martyr behavior to compensate for the guilt he feels because he is angry at being left alone. Denying anger and feeling guilty may be at the root of becoming a martyr.

A husband, left alone through death or divorce, may reason: *She made me suffer deeply by leaving me. It's all her fault that I became physically and emotionally upset. Because of her I lost my job. Here I am, with no job, left to raise two children, and I'm a physical and emotional wreck.*

Or a severe sense of guilt may set in after divorce. A husband may think: *She probably won't survive, now that I've left her. I wonder what's going to happen to the children now that I'm not around to protect them from her.* Anger and guilt become dominant in his thinking and he assumes a martyr's role.

An unmarried mother may feel guilty, angry, rejected, and may experience a bitterness toward men in general. She may also lose some of her friends, finally assume a "what's the use" attitude, and become a martyr.

A single adoptive parent, on the other hand, discovers that being a parent is indeed a big job and finds himself saying, "I don't know why I took on all this responsibility."

Still another may express his anger toward God. *How could You do this to me, God? I love You! Is this the way You show Your love to me? Sometimes I wonder if it's worth it to believe and trust You. You've failed me again.*

So we allow ourselves to become martyrs—full of anger, guilt, defeat, discouragement, and frustration.

Psychosomatic Ailments

"Almost half the patients seen initially by the family doctor in his general practice have symptoms not based on organic disease," says Dr. Quentin Hyder. Repressed anger may manifest itself through psychosomatic ailments such as nausea, indigestion, tension headaches, and hyperventilation.

According to Joel Homer in "The Will to Die" (*Family Health,* February, 1975):

> For twenty years scientists at the University of Rochester have been investigating the consequences of psychological loss on physical disease. In one study they interviewed 51 healthy women who had regular Pap smears. (Each woman showed some suspicious cells in her cervix, but none were cancerous.) During the interviews, the researchers learned that 18 of the women had recently experienced some psychological loss that had produced a feeling of hopelessness. It was predicted that these 18 women would be predisposed to develop cancer. Eleven of them did.

Dr. Karl Menninger in his book *Whatever Became of Sin?* says:

> Each individual exists in a complicated balanced relationship with other persons and things externally, and with intricate parts of himself within. These internal and external parts also attempt to maintain *their* internal and external balances, with constantly changing relationships. Stresses of various kinds bear upon and develop within all of them. All of us make the best possible adaptations to the mishmash of biological and social existence by constantly rear-

ranging ourselves, externally and internally—and sometimes rearranging someone else! Externally we make friend
and foe; we give and take; we approach and retreat. Internally, the many interacting parts and processes of the
human organism try to adapt themselves to the outside situations and events and to the other internal parts and
maintain a fluctuating balance.

The automatic salvaging process can, of course, be overwhelmed. If the tension and disorganization become too
great, the pain will be unbearable, and functioning
seriously impaired. On the other hand, if inner tension becomes too low, growth and adaptation become sluggish and
the organism succumbs in another and more terrible way.
Even the most "normal" individual has his limits of tolerance, his unexpected and disturbing encounters, his hard-
to-bear disappointments, and his inconsolable griefs.
[Footnote to sentence] A "normal" person will possess a
relatively healthy and intact ego, one whose "elasticity" is
not reduced too much by scars and weaknesses and tender
spots and blind spots. Such an ego will have established a
system of relationships with love objects, a network of in-
tercommunication, a program of work satisfactions and
play satisfactions. He will have learned to channel his ag-
gressiveness in the least harmful directions and toward the
most suitable objects. He will have found ways to be creative within the limits of his talents. He will have developed
a love-and-let-love attitude toward the world.

Dr. Hyder, in his book *The Christian's Handbook of Psychiatry,* has the following to say about the effect of crisis on
an individual:

Mucous and ulcerative colitis are frequently caused by or made worse by emotional problems. Guilt, hostility, and resentment also sometimes are seen in these patients. Serious episodes of ulcerative colitis often follow a few days or a few weeks after a significant emotional crisis such as a bereavement, divorce, rejection by a loved one, business failure, financial loss, or threat of serious physical illness. Insecurity and loss of self-esteem are sometimes involved.

It is unwise to tell a single parent or a child, "Come on, now, you're really not sick. It's all in your mind." The symptoms are very real to the individual and could be serious. It's always best to suggest a complete physical checkup. Searching out a counselor who can help the individual recognize why he is feeling as he is and encourage him emotionally and mentally through this crisis period of life is also very important.

June suffered a variety of emotional conflicts for several months after the sudden death of her young husband, Jim. She worried about one physical ailment after another and became convinced she had a malignant tumor. Putting her in the hospital for a complete physical, the doctor assured her that her emotional and physical problems were a result of her response to her husband's death.

Jim had provided abundantly for her and the family, but he had not helped her in her greatest areas of need—to be an independent person and to accept some responsibility. When he died she naturally felt completely inadequate to carry on. She reacted by becoming emotionally and physically sick. Her children continued to reinforce the same kind of behavior by allowing their mother to be dependent on them. Through counseling, the children were urged to encourage their mother to become independent and to learn to accept responsibility herself.

After my own husband's death, I often found my stomach upset and my heart racing; running through my mind were the uncertainties of the days, weeks, months, and years to come. These physical symptoms were just God's way of saying, "Let's take a look at your life and see what we can do to adjust some things. This really isn't the way I want you to live."

Dr. M. L. Ashton, in *A Mind at Ease,* suggests that mental tension is caused by some sort of conflict within the personality of the concerned individual. He lists the results of tension under three categories: mental, physical, and spiritual. Dr. Ashton says: "Results of tension which are primarily mental include insomnia, lack of concentration, a mind which 'goes round in circles,' different forms of hysteria, anxiety states in which the patient is always anxious and apprehensive quite apart from circumstances, and chronic depression." Some physical results of tension are loss of appetite, insomnia associated with anxiety, and palpitations which accompany fear. Dr. Ashton notes that some physical symptoms "can be caused by mental reactions." The stiff-neck pattern relates to "a pain in the neck!"; the chest-tension pattern may be an expression of getting things "off our chests"; and a stomach-tension problem may indicate that we are "sick" of a thing or "fed up!"

In his book Dr. Ashton further points out that tension affects our spiritual life.

Tension robs us of that rest and quietness of heart which is so essential to close communion with God. God says to us, "Be still and know that I am God," but stillness is impossible to the one whose mind and emotions are in a state of tension. Our fellowship with God and our knowledge of God are hindered by tension.

Our witness to the Lord Jesus and our usefulness in His service are marred by tension. Unbelievers are very quick to discern whether Christians have minds at ease and are really resting in the Lord; they are not likely to listen seriously to such invitations as that of the Lord Jesus when He said, "Come unto Me and I will give you rest," if the invitation is passed on to them by those who, though professing to know the Lord, are not displaying in their lives the rest which He gives.

The single parent with behavioral problems causes physical and mental chaos for herself or himself and for the children in the family. Recognition of parental responsibility and reliance on a God who cares are essential for the resolution of problems of parental offenders.

> Seek out a qualified counselor and also have a complete physical checkup.
> Recognize your problems and tensions. Are they affecting your mental, physical, and spiritual well-being?
> Be willing to change. Reread Dr. Menninger's definition of a "normal" person and seek to become that kind of an individual.
> Memorize the following Scriptures:
> For God hath not given us the spirit of fear; but of power, and of love, and of a sound mind.
>
> 2 Timothy 1:7

I will both lay me down in peace, and sleep: for thou Lord, only makest me dwell in safety.

Psalms 4:8

Thou wilt keep him in perfect peace, whose mind is stayed on thee.....

Isaiah 26:3

Suggested Reading

Ashton, M. L. *A Mind at Ease.* Fort Washington, Pa.: Christian Literature Crusade, 1961.

Hyder, O. Quentin. *The Christian's Handbook of Psychiatry.* Old Tappan, N.J.: Fleming H. Revell, 1971.

Maltz, Maxwell. *Psycho-Cybernetics.* New York: Pocket Books, 1970.

McMillan, S. I. *None of These Diseases.* Old Tappan, N.J.: Fleming H. Revell, 1963.

Children have more need of models than of critics.

JOSEPH JOUBERT

11
Living Creatively With Children

God created us to have parents of both sexes—a mother and a father. Appropriate sex identities must be maintained by these parents. They should interact in complementary ways with each other and with their children.

This is the ideal! Unfortunately, we live and function in a less-than-ideal world. Life today includes death, divorce, separation, desertion, unmarried couples cohabitating, unmarried parents, single males and females adopting. Literally millions of children are involved in these diverse living situations.

A few years ago researchers began to study the effect death and divorce had on children. We are now anticipating difficult questions children being brought into these complex living arrangements will ask. And though Paul C. Glick, senior demographer for the United States Bureau of the Census suggests that, "To the extent that the general public becomes adjusted to the prevailing family diversity, children may be expected to grow up believing that such diversity is normal," we may be assured children will continue to ask questions—complicated questions.

Before we discuss living creatively with our children, we need to consider briefly how our children may feel and react to death, divorce, adoption, or being children of an unmarried parent.

Death

Small children have limited ideas about death. They accept it somewhat as a matter of course. Sometimes they feel responsible for the death of a loved one. Children may think that if they are good, the loved one will not die. As they grow older they become more emotional about death. They are very concerned that their mother may die. Children in the seven-year-old to nine-year-old bracket may think of dead people as skeletons or ghosts. One of my nieces, when confronted with the question, "Have you ever seen a dead person before?" answered, "Well, only the ones at the museum, with their skins off." But by nine or ten children are able to understand more about death and realize that when death occurs an individual does not breathe.

Each child will respond differently to death. Much depends on how his family responds to the experience, particularly his remaining parent.

Divorce

Dr. J. Louise Despert, child psychiatrist and author of *Children of Divorce,* says, "It is not divorce, but the emotional situation in the home, with or without divorce, that is the determining factor in a child's adjustment. A child is very disturbed when the relationship between his parents is very disturbed."

Dr. Despert reviewed more than a thousand cases of disturbed children who came to her. She found there were far fewer children of divorce in her group of disturbed children than in the general population; but there was trouble between nearly all of the parents of the disturbed children who were brought to her for help. The problem lies in the unhappiness of the parents, which exists even before the divorce takes place. Dr. Despert calls this "emotional divorce" and says it is more disturbing to a child than the actual divorce.

Dr. Despert gives four guiding principles in discussing divorce with a child of any age:

1. Acknowledge that there has been a decision to separate. He already knows there is trouble, and to talk with you calmly and simply about the impending separation will help relieve his anxiety.
2. Acknowledge that grownups can make mistakes, and that his parents have made them. He must one day accept the fact that his parents are human; it is part of his growing up. You may be hurrying him a little, but the truth is a more durable basis for his confidence in you than a fiction of your godlike perfection which in any case cannot be maintained.
3. Assure him that he is in no way to blame for what has happened between his parents. No matter what may have been said in anger or impatience, the trouble lies only between his parents and quite apart from him. In this way you help to relieve the guilt which most children take upon themselves when there is trouble between their parents. But be careful, in freeing him from blame, that you do not by implication lay the blame upon someone else, that is, upon each other. "Bad" and "good" are words which have no place in this discussion. His parents simply do not get along with each other. This period of your own emotional confusion is no time to make judgments, and certainly not to a child.

4. Finally and most important, assure him in every possible way that despite your differences with each other, you both still love him as you always have.

Adoption

Adopting parents may panic when a child begins to ask questions about his own parents and his past. His curiosity is perfectly natural. Answer his questions matter-of-factly and honestly. It's generally believed that some knowledge of his background is good for an adopted child, when it's a part of his everyday living. It will help him to learn the good points about his biological parents. Obviously, it isn't necessary to go into detail.

Your child may want to know why he was given up for adoption. A general idea may be conveyed, "Your parents couldn't give you the home they wanted to, so they let you come to one that would be better for you."

Since a large percentage of children available for adoption are born to unmarried parents, your child may be one of them, and this information may come to his knowledge. His questions may be tough to handle. Perhaps just letting him know that sometimes people believe they love each other without a formal relationship will satisfy his questioning. This will be an excellent time to provide some sex education by simply sharing with your child that God's plan for a loving relationship between a man and woman is only within the framework of marriage. But your main concern is to demonstrate to your child that you accept and love him for the person he himself is.

Your child may want to see confidential records regarding his past. He needs to be assured that his personal identity will never be erased. Sometime he may need to see these records. Chances are he never will. Answering questions as they arise will probably satisfy him.

It's important to tell a child that he is adopted as soon as he can understand at all. He is bound to find out sometime, and if a relative or playmate tells him, it will come as a shock. The security he needs so much may be destroyed. He may think there is something really awful about being adopted. It's important to be honest. The most important thing you need to share is that you wanted him and you love him.

Unmarried Parent

The questions a child of an unmarried parent ask will undoubtedly be difficult to answer. As with the adopted child, a parent must be as honest as he or she can be without hurting the child. The child will probably wonder why he only has a mother, why his name is the same as his mother's and grandparent's name, why his family is hesitant to talk to him about his birth, why he doesn't know his father's family. Sometimes families of the child of the unmarried parent may deceive the child by saying, "Your father is in the army," or, "He was killed in the war." Honesty is probably the best policy in the long run, even though it may present difficulties. It might even be advisable to simply say, "I made a mistake in getting involved when I was very young. But I love you very much. You are special to me."

You may be asking yourself: *Where do I go from here? How do I live in this less-than-ideal situation? Since statistics are stacked against my family and me, can I prove statistics*

wrong? Can my children live purposeful, fulfilled lives, or will
they suffer emotionally, mentally, intellectually, spiritually, or
physically?

The first and most important step in living creatively is to
learn about God. This should be given top priority in the
single parent's home and can best be accomplished in
everyday situations—through normal conversation, meal-
time prayers, nighttime stories, Christian friends, and
church. A single parent's attitude toward God will be important to a child in forming his own concept of God.

J. B. Phillips, in *Your God Is Too Small,* says:

> But what has this to do with an adequate conception of
> God? This, that the early conception of God is almost in-
> variably founded upon the child's idea of his father. If he is
> lucky enough to have a good father this is all to the good,
> provided of course that the conception of God grows with
> the rest of the personality. But if the child is afraid (or
> worse still, afraid and feeling guilty because he is afraid) of
> his own father, the chances are that his Father in Heaven
> will appear to him a fearful Being. Again, if he is lucky, he
> will outgrow this conception, and indeed differentiate be-
> tween his early "fearful" idea and his later mature concep-
> tion. But many are not able to outgrow the sense of guilt
> and fear, and in adult years are still obsessed with it, al-
> though it has actually nothing to do with their real relation-
> ship with the living God. It is nothing more than a parental
> hangover.

The child who has not had a lasting relationship with a father may find it difficult to relate to a Heavenly Father. He

cannot understand, let alone believe, that God is a God of love and will never fail him.

When a father is gone from the home, a loving, nurturing mother may help her children form a correct concept of God, through the teaching of God's Word, by her own example, and by helping her children find and observe godly male models.

Sociologists have noted that families are more successful in riding out separation if the break is prepared for well in advance. According to E. Reuben Hill ("Social Stresses on the Family"), they have also discovered: "Family adaptability, family integration, affectional relations among family members, good marital adjustment of husband and wife, companionable parent-child relationships, family council type of control in decision-making, social participation of wife, and previous successful experience with crisis were all confirmed as important factors in enabling families to adjust to crisis" (*Social Problems: Persistent Challenges*. Edited by E. C. McDonagh and J. E. Simpson).

Dr. Roger Crook in *An Open Book to the Christian Divorcée* says:

As you face the prospect of rearing your child without the help of his father or mother, you will do well to keep one fact in mind: Your child's needs are exactly the same as the needs of all other children. He needs food, clothing, and shelter. He needs to love and to be loved. He needs friends. He needs adult models from whom he can learn what it means to be a man or what it means to be a woman. He needs an education. He needs a right relationship with God. Your problem is to supply those needs without the help of your husband or wife.

God has not left you helpless in raising your children alone, but will give you strength, courage, finances, and all else required to parent your children successfully.

What are some of the aids we have for living creatively with our children? How do we actually go about it? The following is a list of ten major areas in which you may creatively participate with your children. Listed under each heading are specific activities; many of these I have personally found to be creative outlets for myself and my family.

Reading   From the earliest possible age, children should be exposed to a variety of good reading material. For example: the Bible, Bible stories, poetry, classics, fairy tales, stories rich with traditional warmth and humor, educational material, travel and adventure books, sports, biographies, and picture books. My oldest daughter, at thirty-four, still cherishes an adventure book about Russia, *Old Peter's Russian Tales.* She read and reread the book in childhood and is now sharing it with her own two adopted children.

No child should be without books in our society today. They may be purchased new or secondhand or borrowed from the public library or bookmobile. Books may be handed down from child to child and should be treated with respect and care. Early reading to the child and continued reading by the child are most valuable assets. Teachers from elementary school through college stress the importance of reading to successful scholarship throughout life, and have found good reading habits to be basic to success in any endeavor.

Games   If a parent has actively engaged in playing games with his children from early childhood, they will continue to do so throughout adolescence and even into adulthood. As with books, there is a vast selection available for every age and every pocketbook. There are indoor and outdoor games, educational, fun, technical, mind-expanding, writing, and active games. They may provide entertainment on a rainy day, at a party, and for family fun-time during holiday vacation. Games may often be educational aids in teaching history, math, or spelling; they may also be valuable in teaching cooperation, good sportsmanship, decision making, and in developing a sense of humor. I often found personal delight in playing make-believe or homemade games with my children.

Music   One need not be a musician to share the delights of music with his children. Early exposure to good music will be beneficial throughout life. Children's television programs often use classical and semiclassical music, operas, and marches as backgrounds, and a child thus becomes familiar with a variety of selections in an entertaining way. Children should be encouraged to take music lessons, sing in school and church choral groups, and play in the band or orchestra. Music can be enjoyed individually or as a family. Music was not only a pleasant experience for me but became a means of adding to the family income as I gave private piano lessons. Children who have a variety of interests have less chance of becoming bored. If more than one area is at least partially developed, there will be less trauma should one area of endeavor fail.

Arts and Crafts   The world is an exciting place in which to live today, with a variety of creative crafts everywhere. Anyone, from the youngest child to the oldest grandmother, can find something to do with his or her hands and do it well. My youngest son spent hours painting by number. He also enjoyed his workbench, where he built birdcages and cars. My daughter Sharon delighted in sewing and today is able to produce anything from clothing to curtains to pocketbooks. A walk through the woods will provide leaves, flowers, weeds, and small fruit to make an elegant picture.

Arts and crafts can be a source of entertainment for the entire family as well as an added means of income. Mothers, fathers, and children alike can share in creating a variety of items which may be practical or beautiful.

Organizations   Society is providing more and better organizations to help the single parent and his child. Churches have Boys' Brigade, Pioneer Girls, Awana Clubs, mothers' clubs, singles' groups, young people's organizations, and camps. The YWCA and YMCA offer swimming classes in which everyone can participate. Boy Scouts and Girl Scouts are organizations that are available in every community. Single parents may enjoy becoming leaders in one or more of these groups. The need for vital leaders is great; children love to have their parents become active in such groups. Belonging to social groups provides a variety of friends and activities for children and enlarges the single parent's circle of friends.

Physical Activities   Boys have traditionally been spotlighted in the area of strenuous physical activity, and this activity should rightly continue. Good models for boys, such as coaches, can be a great help to the single parent. Fortunately, the traditional picture of sports being for boys only is changing in today's society, and girls can now enjoy almost every competitive sport—at least through high school. Whatever your views on what sports male and female children should participate in, athletics teach good sportsmanship, how to win and how to lose, cooperation, enthusiasm, skill, stick-to-itiveness and how to perform in public.

One of my sons became proficient in several sports. This was beneficial to him because it provided: a good outlet for pent-up energy, an opportunity to observe and work with adult male models, many hours of hard work, fun, and competition, and success experiences that helped him through difficult adolescent years.

An entire family may be participants or spectators in such sports as swimming, bowling, skiing, ice-skating, and tennis. Single parents should learn enough about several sports so that they can enjoy and discuss them with their children.

Travel Children delight in trips, whether short or long, near or far. If well prepared for, a weekend camping trip will be exciting for the entire family. It's great fun to travel to Detroit or Chicago (or a large city near you) to see a professional ball game, visit the art museum, or attend a concert. Children should be exposed to various modes of travel—car, bus, train, airplane, or boat—and sometimes be allowed to travel alone. Many families enjoy the beautiful world God created by biking to a lake, park, or forest preserve. Much in life is still free of charge—all it takes is a little effort, time, and energy.

Sharing Household Responsibilities It can be fun! Every member of the household should be involved in cleaning the house, washing the clothes, cooking, yard work, shoveling snow, painting, papering, repairing, and carrying out the trash. Children should be taught at an early age to perform simple tasks. Greater responsibility should be added with age. Responsibility can be fun when everyone pitches in; the tasks are soon completed so everyone can relax and have fun. Boys can learn to bake cakes and cookies, make hamburgers, wash and dry clothes, vacuum, and dust the furniture. Girls, on the other hand, need to learn to repair a lamp cord, paint a window, or hammer a nail when necessary. After my husband died, our family ripped up the old carpet (saving thirty dollars), papered the living room, dining room, and one bedroom, painted the other rooms, repaired torn screens, made curtains and bedspreads, antiqued a bedroom set, and then proudly enjoyed our creativity.

Teaching and Learning Social Graces Children need to learn how to keep themselves clean and neat, how to dress for various occasions, and how to carry on a conversation with others—being neither shy or overbearing. Young children should be taken to a variety of places where they can learn how to behave properly in public. In church they need to be quiet and reverent—within reason. In a restaurant they will observe how to eat as ladies and gentlemen, how much to tip the waitress, how to pay the bill, how to seat a lady, and which fork to use. Going to McDonald's will not be particularly beneficial in learning social graces, so once in a while single parents need to save their nickles and dimes to take the family to a special restaurant.

Sharing Preparation for Life's Major Transitions Important events such as entrance to high school, leaving for college, starting a career, and preparing for marriage and family life provide an opportunity for the family to share in the planning.

Preparation for one's entire life begins in the home. This is not only sensible and practical, it is also scriptural. In Deuteronomy 6:6–9 we read:

> And these words, which I command thee this day, shall be in thine heart: And thou shalt teach them diligently unto thy children, and shalt talk of them when thou sittest in thine house, and when thou walkest by the way, and when thou liest down, and when thou risest up. And thou shalt bind them for a sign upon thine hand, and they shall be as frontlets between thine eyes. And thou shalt write them upon the posts of thy house, and on thy gates.

The creative activities of infancy, early childhood, and adolescence which were shared by parent and child should now make the big decisions (college, career, marriage, parenthood) easier for the child becoming an adult.

Dr. Bruce Narramore, in his book *An Ounce of Prevention,* gives us this word of advice:

> From birth onward, our goal should be to free our children from our control and prepare them to accept responsibility for their own decisions. As we are sensitive to their capabilities, our role gradually changes from protector and director to guide and friend. By late adolescence our role should have become largely that of example and friend. Hopefully, we will also be their welcome counselor or experienced guide.

Dr. Frank Cheavens, in his book *Creative Parenthood*, cites a study done in a midwestern town by two behavioral scientists at the University of Chicago, Peck and Havighurst. They were trying to discover why character developed as it did in children and youth in this community of 10,000 people. Five character types developed from the study, but Cheavens reports:

> The most positive character development, perhaps the only truly positive character development, was found in the group designated "rational-altruistic." Parents were consistent, trustful, democratic, and loving. Punishments were not harsh. The authors write, "To be intelligently and effectively ethical it appears necessary to add to this pattern (of love) the element of democracy, the opportunity to experiment in making decisions, and to develop and trade ideas, unafraid, with parents and other family members."

Stanley Coopersmith, in his "Studies in Self-Esteem" (*Scientific American,* February, 1968), found evidence to support what has already been said in this chapter.

> Looking into the backgrounds of the boys who possess high self-esteem, we were struck first and foremost by the close relationships that existed between these boys and their parents. The parents' love was not necessarily expressed in overt shows of affection or the amount of time they spent with their children; it was manifested by interest in the boys' welfare, concern about their companions, availability for discussion of the boys' problems and participation in *congenial joint activities* [author's italics]. The mother knew

all or most of her son's friends, and the mother and father gave many other signs that they regarded the boy as a significant person who was inherently worthy of their deep interest. The family life of the high self-esteem boys was marked not only by the existence of a well-defined constitution for behavior but also by a democratic spirit. . . . It seems safe to conclude that all these factors—deep interest in the children, the guidance provided by well-defined rules of expected behavior, nonpunitive treatment and respect for the children's views—contributed greatly to the development of the boy's high self-esteem.

Living creatively with our children, as single parents, is critical, not only for our own well-being, but for the development of stability and maturity in the lives of our children. The days ahead may bring them experiences that are similar to the ones we have had—perhaps better ones, but perhaps worse. How creatively we have lived with them in their formative years will greatly affect their handling of similar crises which may arise in their own adult lives.

> Prepare children, as much as possible, for any crisis experience.
> Parents need divine guidance in telling their children about death, divorce, adoption, or why they have only one parent.
> Learn about God—by yourself and with your children.
> If the earthly mother or father is gone, provide godly male or female models for children to follow.
> Live creatively with your children. Use the ten suggestions given in this chapter for your own family activities and creativity.

Study suggestions and characteristics given by Dr. Bruce Narramore and Stanley Coopersmith. Strive to incorporate them into your training and living.

Suggested Reading

Adams, Jay E. *Christian Living in the Home.* Nutley, N.J.: Presbyterian and Reformed Publishing.

The American Institute of Family Relations. Publication Number 221: *Short Reading List on Child Guidance.* Los Angeles, Calif. 90027.

———. Publication Number 320: *Short Reading List on Family Recreation.* Los Angeles, Calif. 90027.

Anson, Elva. *How to Keep the Family That Prays Together From Falling Apart.* Chicago: Moody Press, 1975.

Campus Life magazine. P.O. Box 419, Wheaton, Ill. 60187.

Carlton, Anna Lee. *Guidelines for Family Worship.* Anderson, Ind.: Warner, 1964.

Jacobsen, Marion L. *How to Keep Your Family Together and Still Have Fun.* (Original title: *Popcorn, Kites and Mistletoe.*) Grand Rapids: Zondervan, 1972.

LeBar, Lois E. *Family Devotions with School-Age Children.* Old Tappan, N.J.: Fleming H. Revell, 1980.

Lee, Mary P. *Money and Kids: How to Earn It, Save It, and Spend It.* Philadelphia: Westminster Press, 1973.

Mains, Karen B. *Open Heart—Open Home.* Elgin, Ill.: David C. Cook, 1976.

Martin, Dorothy. *Creative Family Worship.* Chicago: Moody Press, 1976.

Mattson, Lloyd D. *Family Camping.* Chicago: Moody Press, 1973.

Narramore, S. Bruce. *A Guide to Child Rearing.* Grand Rapids: Zondervan, 1972.

Narramore, Clyde M. *How to Begin and Improve Family Devotions.* Grand Rapids: Zondervan, 1961.

Schaeffer, Edith. *Hidden Art.* Wheaton, Ill.: Tyndale House, 1971.

————. *What Is a Family?* Old Tappan, N.J.: Fleming H. Revell, 1975.

Sloane, Valeri. *Creative Family Activities.* Nashville: Abingdon, 1976.

Strauss, Richard L. *Confident Children and How They Grow.* Wheaton, Ill.: Tyndale House, 1975.

The church is not a gallery for the exhibition of eminent Christians, but a school for the education of imperfect ones, a nursery for the care of weak ones, a hospital for the healing of those who need assiduous care.

HENRY W. BEECHER

One of the greatest services a church can offer a community is to provide a place for people to be brought to wholeness—to be healed physically, spiritually and emotionally. A place where people are loved, accepted and forgiven.

JERRY COOK
Love, Acceptance and Forgiveness.

12
Society and the Single Parent

Society is faced with a gigantic mission—that of helping millions of single parents and their children establish a new life-style. These people represent a segment of society that has been virtually ignored.

Britton Wood, single adult minister of the Park Cities Baptist Church in Dallas, Texas, had this to say in "The Formerly Married," a message delivered at the Continental Congress on the Family, "The people of God are on the verge of one of the greatest adventures the church has ever known. We are beginning to see all persons—particularly the divorced, widowed, and separated adults—in our midst. Ministry with and to them is the church's new frontier."

"People are fragmented. They are torn. Life doesn't work for them because they are without Jesus," says Jerry Cook in his book *Love, Acceptance and Forgiveness.* "They don't need more programs and more activities," he continues, "they simply need a place to be healed. The place does not have to be fancy. The physical environment need not be impressive. The people don't have to be super-spiritual. They simply need to be real, loving, accepting and forgiving."

Thank God for people who care! I'm afraid, however, all too many Christians, yes, even ministers, lack understanding and compassion regarding people in crisis. I was recently deeply distressed as I learned of one minister who doesn't believe God wants preachers to counsel. He personally feels "tired, unsatisfied and dirty" after hearing people's problems. He does, however, give one afternoon a week to counseling. He also says he would rather handle a thousand people than one or ten. He further contends that ministers are glad to counsel because "they don't have to prepare for it." (Qualified counselors would certainly disagree with him on this point. Good counseling requires much prayer and preparation before, during, and after a time of counseling.) Finally, this minister thinks that a strong pulpit ministry will create a strong church.

I certainly would agree that good preaching is essential to the development of any church. Unfortunately, however, a small percentage of people in crisis enter the church door, so the church's ministry must, of necessity, be broader than just a "pulpit ministry."

Nowhere in the Bible do I find that God considers it a priority to minister to a thousand over one or ten. In fact, genealogies may give credence to the fact that God is interested in all the Jeans and Jims in the world—individuals for whom Christ died. Jesus constantly ministered to individuals (*see* Luke 8:43–56: Christ healed the woman who had an issue of blood for twelve years, then raised Jairus' daughter from the dead). Neither do I find Christ's ministry always within the confines of a "church." Rather, he was a man on the go, meeting the needs of people where they were—geographically, physically, spiritually, and emotionally. And though Christ was the perfect, sinless, Son of God and dealt with some very "dirty" problems, I do not get the impression that he "felt dirty and unsatisfied" after ministering to people. While Jesus hated the sin, He always loved the sinner (*see* John 8:1–11, the story of the woman taken in adultery). After the accusing Scribes and Pharisees left, having their consciences smitten, Jesus "lifted up himself, and saw none but the woman" and said to her, "Woman, where are those thine accusers? Hath no man condemned thee?" She replied, "No man, Lord." Then Jesus said, "Neither do I condemn thee: go, and sin no more." A beautiful picture of a compassionate Christ, and what superb counseling!

Naturally Jesus became tired. Remember, he was human as well as divine. Ministering to needy people took something out of him (Luke 8:46: ". . . I perceive that virtue [strength] is gone out of me") just as it does us.

Imagine, if you can, Christ saying, "Shame on you! How did you ever get in such a mess? I can't deal with your situation now. There are one thousand people waiting to hear me. Come and hear me preach. I'm sure you'll find answers to your problems there. Otherwise, call my secretary and make an appointment for some Thursday afternoon between two and four. That's when I counsel." The Bible, from cover to cover, is a book about people with problems and about a God who is willing to listen, love, correct, heal, and forgive.

If, indeed, you don't feel your calling to be a counseling ministry, how much better to simply say, "I want you to know that I do care about you and will be praying for you. In fact, let's stop right now and pray together." After prayer you might add, "Counseling doesn't seem to be my gift. Preaching is, but I know someone who is an excellent counselor and I'm sure he can help you at this time of crisis in your life. I'd be glad to make the contact for you."

The church obviously has not taken Scripture seriously regarding single parents and their children. There are some one hundred verses in the Bible specifically dealing with widows and orphans. For example:

Exodus 22:22 Ye shall not afflict any widow, or fatherless child.

Deuteronomy 10:18 He doth execute the judgment of the fatherless and widow, and the stranger, in giving him food and raiment.

Deuteronomy 14:29 ... and the stranger, and the fatherless, and the widow, which are within thy gates, shall come, and shall eat and be satisfied; that the Lord thy God may bless thee in all thy work of thine hand which thou doest.

Psalms 146:9 The Lord preserveth the strangers; he relieveth the fatherless and the widow.

Job 29:12, 13 Because I delivered the poor that cried, and the fatherless, and him that had none to help him. The blessing of him that was ready to perish came upon me: and I caused the widow's heart to sing for joy.

James 1:27 Pure religion and undefiled before God and the Father is this, To visit the fatherless and widows in their affliction; and to keep himself unspotted from the world.

Jay E. Adams in his book *Christian Living in the Home* says:

The church of Jesus Christ has failed miserably in helping the single parent. When a woman must raise her children alone without male influence, it is difficult for the child, particularly if he is a boy. It may be that for various reasons she cannot marry again. Thus a covenant child may grow up in the church without a father. The church ought to move in and provide fathering for such children. That child needs to experience something of the fatherly side of a marriage. He needs the men in that congregation. He needs families to invite him over frequently so he can see a family at work; so that he can see the give and take of a husband and a wife. He needs men of the church to take him places—to go fishing with him, hunting with him, to take him camping.

But God is also concerned with those who have suffered the trauma of divorce. Many churches have not, up to this point in time, even acknowledged divorce as a fact of life. With the spiraling divorce rate, we can no longer ignore the divorced in our society and in our churches.

Britton Wood, in the booklet *The Formerly Married,* made an important statement regarding divorce, "The issue is not whether persons should or should not divorce. God's intention in marriage is consistent. The fact is that people are divorced and will continue to divorce. Our concern as the church must be how to minister to these broken lives."

In his book *Guilt and Grace,* Dr. Paul Tournier told this story of a conversation between himself and another Christian doctor.

During our cruise to the North Cape last year I was leaning on the rail one day watching the wonderful Norwegian landscape slip by, with its incredibly green islands and shores contrasting with the great glaciers which come down almost to the sea. A doctor passed in silence, and stood leaning against the same rail beside me, studying the same spectacle. After a moment or two he said, "I'm quite upset. I have just been told that one of our colleagues here has been divorced and remarried. Is it true?" "Yes," I said. After a further silence he went on, "How is it possible? How can you agree to his taking his place among us Christian doctors?" I said nothing for the moment. Then my friend added, "Do you not believe that divorce is disobedience to God? a sin?"—"Certainly," I said, "but if we could have only sinless men among us, there would be no one here; at any rate, I should not be here. We are all alike, we are all forgiven sinners." A long silence followed. My friend went away. Later he returned, "You are right," he said briefly, "now I know what grace means."

Certainly the church has not touched the tip of the iceberg regarding ministry to unmarried parents, single adoptive parents, and their children. Indeed, society can still be cruel to a child born to unmarried parents, labeling him *illegitimate* or worse yet, a *bastard* (this happened to two people I know personally). I was stunned at the response of one individual after I proudly shared with her that my oldest daughter and her husband had adopted a beautiful racially mixed child. "I think that's awful," she said, "I don't know how anyone could do that."

Pastors, youth workers, and counselors will find the contact with people after any crisis experience valuable—not only for the individuals ministered to, but also for themselves and their church. This may be a time to have single-

parent seminars, Bible-study groups, and possibly a Single
Parent Sunday. There are many ways that a pastor and his
congregation can minister after a time of crisis.

One church in the Chicago area asked me to put on a Solo
Parents Workshop. It was held from 10:00 A.M. to 4:00 P.M.,
one Saturday in the church. The three-dollar charge included the workshop, lunch, and baby-sitting for children
through elementary-school age. The program for the day
looked like this:

1. **Dealing with emotions—yours and your children's**
     Living through the crisis cycle
     Handling your fears
     What to do with anger, guilt
     Coping with the transition period
2. **Getting practical help**
     Obtaining job training
     Selecting and finding a job
     The role of the church
     Helps from society
     Managing your finances
3. **Living creatively with your children**
     Financial adjustments
     Having fun together
     Accepting responsibilities in the home
4. **Learning to appreciate the single life-style**
     Finding a place where you fit
     Developing yourself
     Learning self-acceptance
     Making sexual adjustments
     The will of God

The day was well received by about forty men and women who were either divorced or widowed. The church had advertised through newspapers, radio, and church newsletters. People came from various churches and traveled many miles to attend. The church plans a follow-up seminar and has already begun weekly Bible classes for single parents.

Jay Adams, in his book *Competent to Counsel,* has this to say concerning the role of the pastor:

> Grief offers an important opportunity for a pastor to reorient lives according to Biblical patterns. Death demands changes; why shouldn't those changes be in the direction of greater devotion to Christ? When one loses a job, when a divorce ruptures a home, when a child gets into serious trouble, when somehow one loses face, when his life seems to be falling apart, when a client is so deeply depressed that he doesn't know where to turn next, the nouthetic counselor senses an important opportunity to serve Christ. When viewed positively, disintegration of the past may be considered an advantage. If the situation is handled properly, when one's life is disintegrated it can be altered much more readily, much more rapidly, and much more radically along Biblical lines than at any other time.

Single parents are a minority group. As with all minority groups, society will have to be educated regarding the needs that are prevalent in the single-parent world.

Many organizations, services, books, and pamphlets are available to help the single parent. I have listed some of these services and resources on the following pages and hope that you may find the suggestions helpful as you adjust to a new life-style.

Fellowship Groups

Single Parent Christian Fellowship   Public sessions meet once a month in Minneapolis and Saint Paul, Minnesota. Reach Out therapy groups (twenty to forty people, in five different groups) meet once a week to help single parents adjust to divorce and widowhood. These groups are also designed to help facilitators learn to conduct group therapy sessions. Besides the public sessions and group therapy, social and fellowship activities are held each month. A newsletter is published monthly, not only informing members of events, but including articles and other helpful information relative to single parents. Request How-To-Packet to help you organize a single-parent group in your location.

Contact:

> Quentin Alfors
> The Greater Minneapolis Association of Evangelicals
> 6108 Excelsior Blvd.
> Minneapolis, Minnesota 55416

The Sisterhood of Black Single Mothers, Inc.   This is a self-help organization comprised of black women who are raising children alone. Membership is open to women who are separated, divorced, widowed, and mothers who were never married. Objectives are: (1) to encourage a positive self-image of the black single mother and instill in her the determination, awareness, and strength to raise her children in a positive manner, (2) to provide communication between black single mothers and people who have direct influence on their lives (such as social workers, employers, teachers, and so on), and (3) to enable mothers to "help themselves" by providing information and referrals in areas of housing, training, jobs, and education.

The Sisterhood of Black Single Mothers, Inc.
1360 Fulton Street, Room 423
Brooklyn, New York 11216

Youth Awareness Project (Affiliated with the Sisterhood of Black Single Mothers) The Youth Awareness Project is geared to young people twelve to eighteen years old and their families. Objectives are: (1) to provide teen parents with a healthy basis from which to gain incentive, information, and more productive lives, (2) to reduce pregnancy and abortion and repeated-pregnancy rate among teenagers in Central Brooklyn Community, through practical information and awareness, (3) to expose teens to a broad cultural experience, (4) to introduce new positive concepts of male-female identification, (5) to allow greater family harmony via the involvement of the nuclear and extended family of the teen, (6) to offer viable alternatives to the negativity currently existing as a result of minimal self-pride, (7) to teach respect and responsibility in matters relating to sex, and (8) to help youth establish positive goals in both teen parents and teens who are not parents. Write:

Youth Awareness Project
1360 Fulton Street, Room 423
Brooklyn, New York 11216

Service Organizations

Evangelical Child and Family Agency ECFA is a private, nonprofit child welfare agency, licensed by the Illinois Department of Children and Family Services. It is an evangelical Christian organization serving the community through the programs of adoption, foster-family care, services to unmarried parents, and family counseling.

Contact:

ECFA
1530 North Main Street
Wheaton, Illinois 60187

North American Council on Adoptable Children, Inc. The Committee for Single Adoptive Parents has been operating since 1973 as an information service to prospective and actual single adoptive parents, with the following goals: (1) to support the right of adoptable children to loving families, regardless of any difference in race, creed, color, national origin, or of any handicap the children may have, (2) to serve members with information and assistance, (3) to inform public and private agencies of legislation and research applying to single-person adoption. The Committee for Single Adoptive Parents makes the following services available to prospective single parents: *Membership,* which entitles you to receive the Source List and its updates, listing agency or direct sources of adoptable children in the United States and abroad who will accept single applicants. Membership term is approximately eighteen months; the fee is $10.00. *Handbook for Single Adoptive Parents* available for $6.00.

Write:

North American Council on Adoptable Children, Inc.
3900 Market Street, Suite 247
Riverside, California 92501

Family Counseling

American Institute of Family Relations This organization offers several valuable services such as counseling, classes, workshops, and literature. Group and individual counseling is available for the widowed or divorced and parents concerned with child rearing. Examples of courses offered are: Training in Communication Skills, Your Family and You, Successful Parenthood, and Nutrition for the Family. There are workshops for persons concerned over family relationships and for people going through crisis experiences.

Family Life is the institute's bimonthly bulletin. This publication brings to the reader articles on current trends regarding families, news notes from all over the world, information on new pamphlets, and critical reviews of the latest important books on pertinent subjects. The institute also provides more than a hundred pamphlets on subjects such as: part-time jobs for women, handling finances, fun with children, family teamwork, single parenthood, and a reading list on the single woman (including widowed and divorced).

For information regarding these services write to:

Dr. Paul Popenoe
The American Institute of Family Relations
5287 Sunset Boulevard
Los Angeles, California 90027

Narramore Christian Foundation   Write to:

> Dr. Clyde Narramore
> 1409 North Walnut Grove Avenue
> Rosemead, California 91770

Referrals   The following agencies will refer you to a counseling service in your area:

> Family Service Association of America
> 44 East 23rd Street
> New York, New York 10010

> The United Way of America
> 801 North Fairfax
> Alexandria, Virginia 22314

Consumer Information

Consumer Information Center   This center provides an index of selected federal publications of consumer interest. The small pamphlets are available free, or at minimal cost, and cover a range of topics. For example, some titles are: *Insurance for Renters and Homeowners, Shopping for Credit Can Save You Cash, Car Care and Service, Your Right to Credit* (credit for women), *Finding the Best Day Care for Your Children, One-Parent Families, Get Credit for What You Know* (how to get high school and college credit without formal schooling), *Guide to Choosing a Vocational School, Shopping for Educational Services, What Is Your Food Bill?* (tips for cutting your grocery bill), *Used Furniture* (how to select serviceable, economical, secondhand furniture), *Rent or Buy? When You Move—Do's and Don'ts, Sim-*

ple Plumbing Repairs, A Working Woman's Guide to Her Job Rights. For a catalog and further information write to:

> Consumer Information
> Public Documents Distribution Center
> Pueblo, Colorado 81009

U.S. Department of Health, Education, and Welfare   *One-Parent Families* booklet and other publications may be received from:

> U.S. Department of Health, Education, and Welfare
> Office of Human Development and
> Child Development
> Washington, D.C. 20201

Dale Carnegie Courses   This is an adult program designed to develop skill in human relations, self-confidence, and potential for leadership. Many people left alone through death or divorce suffer from a poor self-image. Others will be looking for a job for the first time in their life. The Dale Carnegie Course will help develop confidence and skill to continue life on a positive note. The objectives of the Dale Carnegie Course are to: develop more self-confidence, develop your human relations and leadership ability, develop your ability to speak more effectively to groups, be more convincing in selling your ideas to others, sell yourself more effectively to others, develop more enthusiasm in yourself and others, break the worry habit, increase your income potential. For information write to:

Dale Carnegie Courses, International Headquarters
1475 Franklin Avenue
Garden City, New York 11530

Local Junior Colleges   Junior colleges provide a wealth of subjects that will be helpful to the single parent, and enrollment fees are reasonable. Our local college offers such subjects as: I've Got to Get Organized, The Handywoman Workshop, Back to School, Career Development, Starting Your Own Business, Making Your Money Work for You, and Single Again.

School and Career Guides   Books such as these may be found in the high-school counselor's office, the public library, or they may be purchased: *Lovejoy's College Guide* lists colleges and universities by states. Under each college information as to number of students, costs, programs offered, and accreditation is given.

Lovejoy's Career and Vocational School Guide will provide similar information on career-oriented schools.

The Occupational Outlook Handbook is published by the U.S. Department of Labor, Bureau of Labor Statistics. This book lists many specific occupations and gives information regarding the nature of the job, places of employment, training and qualifications required, advancement opportunities, employment outlook, and the range of earnings.

Career Counseling Centers   Career counseling centers usually offer educational and career counseling. They may help an individual learn how to write an effective resumé, how to ask for a raise, or how to deal with on-the-job problems. Lists of career and educational counseling centers may be obtained by request:

> *Continuing Education Programs and Services for Women*
> Women's Bureau
> U.S. Department of Labor, Employment Standards Administration
> Washington, D.C. 20210
> Free

> *Catalyst National Network of Local Resource Centers*
> Catalyst
> 14 E. 60th Street
> New York, New York 10022
> Free

> *Report on Fifty Selected Centers Offering Career Counseling Services for Women*
> Education Development Centers
> 55 Chapel Street
> Newton, Massachusetts 02160
> $2.00

Financial Planning

American Association of Credit Counselors Write for information regarding your local agency.

> American Association of Credit Counselors
> 912 South Woodward Avenue, Suite 200
> Birmingham, Michigan 48011

Household Finance Corporation Management Program For over forty-eight years, HFC's Money Management program has helped individuals and families manage their financial affairs more effectively. Money Management Booklets Library is available for $5.00. Twelve booklets are included in an attractive box. Titles are: *Your Financial Plan, Managing Your Credit, Children's Spending, Your Food Dollar, Your Clothing Dollar, Your Housing Dollar, Your Home Furnishing Dollar, Your Equipment Dollar, Your Shopping Dollar, Your Automobile Dollar, Your Recreation Dollar,* and *Your Savings and Investment Dollar. A Guide for Teaching Money Management* is also available for $.50.

Order from:

> Household Finance Corporation
> 2700 Sanders Road
> Prospect Heights, Illinois 60070

Books on Finances:

> *Financial Planning Guide for Your Money Matters*
> Malcolm MacGregor
> Bethany House
> Minneapolis, Minnesota
> Published 1977

> *A Kid's Guide to Managing Money*
> Joy Wilt
> Educational Products Division
> Word Books
> Waco, Texas
> Published 1979

How To Succeed With Your Money
George M. Bowman
Moody Press
Chicago, Illinois
Published 1978

Christian Financial Concepts
Larry Burkett
Available through your Christian bookstore

You Can Beat the Money Squeeze
George and Marjean Fooshee
Fleming H. Revell
Old Tappan, New Jersey
Published 1980

Money, A Woman's Guide to Financial Planning
Women's Division
Institute of Life Insurance
277 Park Avenue
New York, New York

How to Get Your Money's Worth
Better Business Bureau
A Benjamin Company/Rutledge Book
New York, New York

Resource Material

Solo Magazine
8740 E. 11th Street, Suite Q
Tulsa, Oklahoma 74112

Solo magazine is a Christian magazine for single adults
and a bimonthly publication of Solo Ministries, Inc. Solo

Ministries is an interdenominational Christian movement working with churches and other Christian organizations to win, build, and bring single adults into a personal relationship with the Lord Jesus Christ. *Solo* is an excellent magazine, which has information on conferences, seminars, travel tours, books, helps, vacation guides, many articles that the single parent will find helpful.

> Bear Valley Baptist Church
> 2600 South Sheridan
> Denver, Colorado 80227

Bear Valley Baptist Church is imaginatively designed to include a variety of ministries that exist outside the normal church structure such as (1) counseling ministry—a ministry helping hurting people and training others to help, (2) health-care ministry—a ministry for the promotion and maintenance of health, (3) life unlimited—a ministry of love and practical help to unwed mothers, (4) MOPS, Mothers of preschoolers, (5) Bear Valley Singles—a specialized ministry to Denver's single adults. Write for literature that may be helpful in structuring a similar ministry in your community.

Tape Ministry   Fourteen Ways to Help Your Single Adult Ministry: Tapes from the first National Conference on Helping Today's Church Effectively Minister with Single Adults. Titles such as: *Defining Your Single Adult Ministry, If I Had to Do It Over Again, For the Widowed, Remarriage Education, Successful Sunday School Programming for Single Adults.* Available from:

Solo House
1650 S.E. Washington Blvd.
Bartlesville, Oklahoma 74003

Books to Help the Single Parent

Single Parents and the Public Schools
Phyllis L. Clay
National Committee for Citizens in Education
410 Wilde Lake Village Green, Suite 410
Columbia, Maryland 21044
$4.25

The Feminine Fix-It Handbook
Kay B. Ward
Grosset and Dunlap
New York, New York
1972

How to Get Control of Your Life and Time
Alan Lakein
New American Library
New York, New York
1974

Do It Now: How to Stop Procrastinating
William J. Knaus
Prentice-Hall
Englewood Cliffs, New Jersey
1979

Leave Your House in Order. A Guide to Planning your Estate.
John G. Watts
Tyndale House
Wheaton, Illinois
1980

Take Charge: Success Tactics for Business and Life
John K. Cannie
Prentice-Hall
Englewood Cliffs, New Jersey
1980

Strategy for Living: How to Make the Best Use of Your Time and Abilities
Edward R. Dayton and Ted W. Engstrom
Regal Books
Glendale, California
1976

Getting Organized
Stephanie Winston
Warner Books
New York, New York
1980

Full-Time Living
Charlotte Hale Allen
Fleming H. Revell
Old Tappan, New Jersey
1978

Alone and Alive (also available in tapes, with study notes)
Dr. Richard D. Dobbins
Emerge Ministries, Inc.
1815 West Market St.
Akron, Ohio 44313

Getting in Touch (also available in tapes, with study notes)
Dr. Richard D. Dobbins
Emerge Ministries, Inc.
1815 West Market St.
Akron, Ohio 44313

Understanding Your Temperament (This book includes a temperament inventory you can take and score yourself. It is very helpful in learning to understand yourself.)
Robert J. Cruise and W. Peter Blitchington
Andrews University Press
Berrien Spring, Michigan 49104

A brochure, "Affirmation on the Family," was published by the *Continental Congress on the Family*. The brochure included a statement on the family and the church. The message is so important that I believe it may be helpful to many churches who are attempting to bring our families back to God. While this statement was meant for the traditional family, I believe it may be used as a guide for the single-parent family as well. The bracketed sections are my additions to emphasize the necessity for churches to consider single-parent families.

The [Single-Parent] Family and the Church

"The [single-parent] family has need of continuing support from other families and from individuals within the church. The local church is a company of believers who exist for fellowship, worship, teaching, and the development of spiritual gifts to the end that God will be glorified and the body of Christ edified. As part of the universal body of Christ, the local church is an extended family composed of nuclear families, [single-parent families] and individuals who are living apart from nuclear families. The church exists to support, nurture, and equip individuals and families [*including single-parent families*] for growth in discipleship (including evangelism) and effective functioning." Churches need to minister to single-parent families in creative ways which build church and family unity, educate single-parent families in effective family living, assist family members in their spiritual and personal growth, and give support in times of stress and special need.

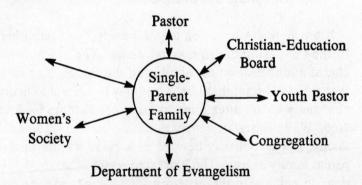

*The whole church can work together to help
the single-parent family*

If you have built castles in the air, your work
need not be lost; there is where they should be.
Now put foundations under them.

HENRY DAVID THOREAU

13
Single Isn't So Bad, After All!

Human tendency is to look at our own limited abilities and resources. If we each could peek over God's shoulder and read the remaining pages of our own book of life, we might be stirred with the excitement of God's dynamic power and what He has yet in mind for us.

God has more confidence in us and knows our potential far better than we do. He has a specific plan and purpose for our lives and will fulfill that plan. To top it off, He has given us the exact qualities needed to fulfill His plan and purpose.

Do you realize, as a single parent, the dynamic power that is available to you or the potential God has in mind for you and your children?

In Philippians 4:13 we read about Paul and his source of power: "I can do all things through Christ which strengtheneth me." Or, to put it another way, I am almighty in the Christ who continually keeps pouring His power in me. This same strength and power is available to you also. Paul was confident and strong because he was plugged into the greatest source of power available. Psalms 23:3 says: "He restoreth my soul. . . ." In other words, God "recharges" our batteries.

We can be "no limit" single parents who move to the farthest edges of our potential and are plugged into the source of dynamic power—God!

God made you a person of unique worth and has given you special gifts so you can make a contribution to the family you've been left to raise alone. You are an original creation—God's masterpiece. He has a master plan for your life as His special creation. Can you not trust Him with your life as a single parent? God knows the story of your life from beginning to end. After all, He wrote it! He will lead you step-by-step, with or without a partner.

The time of rehabilitation is a great time to look at abilities and potentials not yet tapped. They've been lying dormant, just waiting for such a time to blossom. "Nothing ventured, nothing gained" is an old adage that bears consideration. We can wallow in self-pity—"poor little me"—or we can get on our feet, set our mental gears in motion, straighten our spines, and begin to do the things we've always wished we could.

I often think of the story of Moses in the Old Testament. You remember: God told Moses he was going to lead the children of Israel. Moses said to God, "I can't." Does that sound familiar? God said, "Now Moses, who made your mouth? Did not I? Now you *go*, and I will be with your mouth and put the words in your mouth that you are supposed to say." (*See* Exodus 4:11, 12.) Moses again said, "I can't." God must become terribly disgusted with us when He tells us to do something, says He will be with us, and we stand there and say we can't.

Another passage in Scripture that has helped me through some troubled times is the story found in Mark 4:35–41. Jesus said, "Let us go to the other side of the lake." (*See* verse 35.) A great storm arose, and the disciples became very frightened. They cried, "Master, don't you care that we are going to perish?" They forgot that Jesus had told them, "Let *us* go to the *other side.*" God never tells us to go anywhere or do anything unless He will be with us or help us.

Though the storms of life rage about us and we cannot see the other shore or a glimmer of hope, we know that Christ stands with open arms saying, "Peace, be still, my child, for I am with you. Keep your mind on Me, and you will not fall."

My fears will not be as great now as I view circumstances that appear to be in reverse, for I can view them as stepping-stones, blessings in disguise. "God has begun to give . . . I must begin to possess." (*See* Deuteronomy 2:31.) This promise I can claim as I continue to know more of the riches of God's love and grace as expressed in Ephesians 3:20: "Now unto him that is able to do exceeding abundantly above all that we ask or think, according to the power that worketh in us." This promise is for me—and you—as a single parent. I cannot begin to imagine the magnitude of the promise—but I can claim it. That is all God asks.

Can you accept this time in your life as a time when you can develop as an individual and become creatively YOU in a new way? Can you accept the idea that you are where God wants you right now and, as a loving God, He wants the very best for both you and your family?

I must admit that I wasn't too fond of God's plan for my life when I learned of my husband's impending death. It really didn't make sense to me at all. I questioned: *Why did I receive Christ as my Saviour when I was just ten years old, give myself to God for Christian service, prepare in a Christian school, serve Him with joy, and then have to have it all crumble beneath me?*

Fifteen years later—after joys, sorrows, heartaches, and mistakes—I can see a beautiful pattern behind me. Though I do not know my future, I can say I've come a long way. I know God has a continuing plan for my life, as in the past, and His way is best for me.

I can personally say that God intricately planned—and is still working out—every detail of my life and the life of each member of my family.

For example, after my husband became ill, he worked until he could work no longer. God knew what our financial needs would be after my husband's death. After checking to see how many credits he had in social security, we discovered he had exactly enough—no more or no less—to receive social-security benefits during his illness. The children would also receive benefits after his death. God knew when my husband would become ill, how long he would be able to work, when he would become completely disabled, when he would die, and that we would need the financial aid supplied by social security. Intricate? Of course, God is a God of intricacies.

After my husband's death I wanted to return to Christian work. But God had a plan for me that included working in industry and a public-school system for fifteen years. He knew I needed this exposure and training to prepare me for the work He had especially in mind for me.

My goal through the years had been to become a counseling dean in a Christian school. After working almost ten years in industry and getting two daughters started on their way to college, I decided to return to college, too, to prepare myself for a counseling ministry.

However, even after ten years, God was not finished with my preparation. I had been promoted up through several departments in industry and finally worked in personnel. Our main responsibilities were in management development, recruiting, and scholarships. We recruited at seventy major colleges and universities.

The training received during five years in personnel work (particularly regarding colleges) was invaluable to my future work. They were difficult years, but God knew they were essential to fulfill His plan for my life.

An opportunity then occurred for me to become dean of women at a Christian college, while pursuing my own degree. I was delighted! I immediately put my house up for sale, began looking for a house to rent or buy in the new location, and resigned my job in industry.

Two weeks before my position in industry was to terminate, I still had no buyer for my house, no house in the new location, and my son Stan was most unhappy about the prospective move.

Praying, I said, "God, I don't know what You want me to do, but You do. Help me make the right decision."

With the possibility of no job in two weeks and feeling rather low because I could not proceed with *my* plans, I wrote to the college and said, "I cannot come. God has closed every door."

Within a few days a job opened up in the office of the superintendent of our public-school system. The position involved working with federal programs, adult education, and publication of a monthly school newsletter that went into some three thousand homes in our community. This job proved to be just what I needed to continue preparation for my future work in education and counseling.

Intricate! Of course, God delights in intricacies. I had become rather secure with my job in industry, and God took the long way around to "get me out." He also gave me some interesting faith lessons along the way. I met people to whom I could minister. And Stan was delighted that we were going to stay in the community where he had grown up. He was just starting tenth grade when I began my job in the school. I was able to share in his successes and failures in athletics, academics, and personal relationships throughout his high-school years. I believe he would have left home had I moved to the new community. He was struggling enough to find himself, without my uprooting him from familiar territory and friends. I could wait—he could not.

During the three years I worked at the school, I did most of the editing of the monthly newsletter. For many years I had been interested in writing. Now God was giving me an opportunity to do what I wanted to do—and to get paid for it at that!

A year before Stan graduated from high school I began once again to correspond with various colleges. I put out the fleece so to speak. When writing colleges I asked: How many credits will you give me for the schooling I've already had? and, Do you have a job available in the Student Affairs Office?

After hearing from several colleges, one responded favorably. I would receive a good number of credits, and a job would be available in the Student Affairs Office when I was ready to make the move. God answered my prayer exactly. Yes, God deals in intricacies! Again and again He proved His "exceeding abundantly above all" I could ask or think.

I put my house up for sale one Friday in January. During the three years I was waiting for Stan to graduate from high school, we had remodeled the kitchen and bathroom and redecorated every other room in the house. We did much of the work ourselves as a family—painting, papering, and repairing. The house looked very nice. That Friday the real-estate salesman said, "I have a young couple who are look-ing for a house like yours. They want to see it on Monday."

Monday afternoon I called the realtor. "They want your house," he said, "and they gave me seven hundred dollars as down payment. You may stay in the house until June." We did not have to do one more thing to the house. The loan the buyers applied for went through without a hitch. Yes, God deals in intricacies!

That fall Stan started as a freshman at a state university; my daughter, Sharon, was a senior at a Christian college, and I began college as a junior.

I took a two-thousand-dollar cut in pay to go back to school and to work for the college. This seems to be the story of my life—going backward to go forward. I had taken a cut when I left industry to work in the public school; but almost immediately my salary had been raised beyond what I had received in industry. I knew God would provide.

Sure enough, one day the dean of students asked me, "Virginia, how would you like to be resident director of one of the men's dormitories? It will be good experience for you, plus providing room, board, and some financial remunera-tion."

I had considered being resident director of a women's dormitory—but men? Well, it didn't take me long to decide that this was God's will. I accepted the job and was the envy of most women on campus. Living with a hundred men under one roof!

For two years—summer, fall, winter, and spring—I took from six to ten hours of classwork in college, worked full-time as secretary to the dean of students, was resident director of a men's dormitory and was, of course, a parent. And a single parent at that!

But they were two of the happiest, busiest years of my life!

I graduated in May, 1973, at forty-nine years of age, with academic honors. God did provide for me—*exceeding, abundantly,* and *above* my expectations.

To top it off, the first article I had ever written was published in June, 1973, one month after graduation. It was entitled "God's Dynamic Power" and was published in *Christian Life* magazine.

The week after the article was published, I spoke for a Christian Business Women's luncheon in the city where we had lived for fifteen years. It was here my husband had suffered and died; it was here where I had worked in industry and the public school. I knew many of the women who were present at the luncheon because my husband and I had both spoken in many of the churches in the area. Several women from industry and the public-school system were also present for the luncheon.

Best of all, the man for whom I had worked in personnel came to see me before the luncheon to congratulate me on graduation, my new position as dean of women in a Christian college, and my recently published article.

He also shared his recent sorrow with me. With tears in his eyes, he said, "Two weeks ago I put my wife in the hospital. She does not know any of us. The day my daughter came down to help me put my wife in the hospital, her husband died of a heart attack. Virginia, I know you had a source of strength and confidence during Stan's illness. My daughter and I want to read your article. Perhaps it will help us in our sorrow."

Though I was deeply grieved over his heartache, I

thanked God because I had often felt, during my husband's long illness and after his death, that I was not revealing much strength or courage.

I came to understand the verses in 2 Corinthians 1:3, 4 in a more complete way: "Blessed be God, even the Father of our Lord Jesus Christ, the Father of mercies, and the God of all comfort; Who comforteth us in all our tribulation, that we may be able to comfort them which are in any trouble, by the comfort wherewith we ourselves are comforted of God."

It takes courage to trust God—to walk with Him where He leads. But God gives us courage and wants us to be successful. He tells us in Joshua 1:8, 9: ". . . observe to do according to all that is written therein: for then thou shalt make thy way prosperous, and then thou shalt have good success. Have not I commanded thee? Be strong and of a good courage; be not afraid, neither be thou dismayed: for the Lord thy God is with thee whithersoever thou goest."

The world, to me, is a more exciting place to live in now than it was fifteen, twenty, or thirty years ago—though I found it exciting then. I realize how much I have learned, but how little I really know about this vast world which God has given us to enjoy. In spite of some unbearable problems I have experienced, I find the future to be hopeful.

Life is a series of closely woven events that can become a beautiful pattern in God's plan for us. Though I have not always liked what has been "woven," it has been good for me. I can now understand my own self better; I can certainly sympathize and empathize with others in a way I could not have done if this intricate pattern had not been woven.

First and foremost, I believe a personal relationship with Jesus Christ is essential to a good life. Then we must constantly strive to remain positive in our relationships to God, to ourselves, and to others. We need to have a good self-image because we are made in the "image of God"—to do otherwise would be to portray a negative God. We need: to be always learning, seeking to become more knowledgeable of God's universe and of the people in it; to learn to work and live in the world without becoming a "part" of it, rather drawing the world to Christ through our lives; to be diligent, persistent, and consistent in our daily Christian life, without becoming determinists or dogmatists; to be able to sympathize and empathize with others, to share joys and sorrows, to be able to laugh and cry; to be independent, but dependent; and to become more like Christ. This is my philosophy! "For me to live is Christ, and to die is gain" (Philippians 1:21).

I respect the man who knows distinctly what he wishes. The greater part of all the mischief in the world arises from the fact that men do not sufficiently understand their own aims.

JOHANN VON GOETHE

14
The "Me" I Want to Be

You've gone through the emotional trauma of facing the truth that you are now a single parent. You realize your children also grieve during and after crisis; you've discovered the various stages of the crisis cycle and decided where you've been, where you are now; and, hopefully, you have some idea of where you want to go. You've also recognized the importance of heeding emotions and what to do about them. You've admitted that there is an adjustment to be made sexually, that transitions take time, that single parents often behave unacceptably, that you can live creatively with your children, and that society is finally responding to the needs of the single parent.

"Great," you say, "but where do I go from here? How do I make all this information work for me and my family?"

First of all, you need to ask yourself the question, *Do I really want to move ahead, or am I using a dozen excuses to keep myself bogged down?*

Perhaps you are using one or more of the following defense mechanisms to keep you immobilized:

> My children wouldn't like it.
> Well, that's the way I am.
> My family needs me.
> I've been out of it too long.

I could try, but. . . .
I'm afraid other people wouldn't approve of what I'm
    doing.
I wouldn't dare take a risk. That area is unknown to
    me.

If you are uncertain, you need to take a second look at yourself, especially as God sees you. The Single-Parent's Inventory at the end of this chapter may help you to establish some goals and motivate you to move forward with God.

John Powell, in his book *The Secret of Staying in Love,* says:

The essential sadness of our human family is that very few of us even approach the realization of our full potential. I accept the estimate of the theoreticians that the average person accomplishes only 10% of his promise. He sees only 10% of the beauty in the world around him. He hears only 10% of the music and poetry in the universe. He smells only a tenth of the world's fragrance, and tastes only a tenth of the deliciousness of being alive. He is only 10% open to his emotions, to tenderness, to wonder and awe. His mind embraces only a small part of the thoughts, reflections, and understanding of which he is capable. His heart is only 10% alive with love. He will die without ever having really lived or really loved.

Single parent, will you take God's hand and allow Him to lead you into the future? He is waiting for you to do so!

And I said to the man who stood at the gate of the year: "Give me a light that I may tread safely into the un-

known." And he replied: "Go out into the darkness and put
your hand into the hand of God. That shall be to you better
than light and safer than a known way." So I went forth,
and finding the Hand of God, trod gladly into the night.
And He led me towards the hills and the breaking of day in
the lone East.

MINNIE LOUISE HASKINS
God Knows

A Single Parent's Inventory

How does God see you?
> *Psalm 139; Isaiah 43* List six ways from each
> reference.

How do you see yourself?
> List six strengths, assets, and abilities.
> List six weaknesses.

What does God expect you to do?
> *Joshua 1:5–9; Ephesians 5:15–17; Psalms 90:12*
> List several expectations.

What does God say you can become?
> *Joshua 1:8*

What goals have you set for yourself?
> List short-term goals and when you expect to
> reach them.
> List long-term goals and when you expect to reach
> them.

What steps do you need to take to reach these goals?
> List these steps for your short-term goals.
> List these steps for your long-term goals.

**What are some difficulties you must face in reaching
these goals?**

What can you do to overcome these difficulties?
What are some ways God wants you to minister to others?

    Isaiah 61:1, 2; 2 Corinthians 1:3, 4   List at least six.